THE NARRATIVE POEMS OF
PERCY BYSSHE
SHELLEY

THE NARRATIVE POEMS OF

PERCY BYSSHE SHELLEY

ARRANGED IN CHRONOLOGICAL
ORDER
WITH AN INTRODUCTION BY
C. H. HERFORD, F.B.A.
LITT.D.

VOLUME II

AT THE FLORENCE PRESS
LONDON: CHATTO & WINDUS
M·CM·XXVII

CONTENTS

PRINCE ATHANASE

A Fragment

PART I

THERE was a youth, who, as with toil and travel,
Had grown quite weak and gray before his time;
Nor any could the restless griefs unravel

Which burned within him, withering up his prime
And goading him, like fiends, from land to land.
Not his the load of any secret crime,

For nought of ill his heart could understand,
But pity and wild sorrow for the same;—
Not his the thirst for glory or command,

Baffled with blast of hope-consuming shame;
Nor evil joys which fire the vulgar breast,
And quench in speedy smoke its feeble flame,

Had left within his soul their dark unrest:
Nor what religion fables of the grave
Feared he,—Philosophy's accepted guest.

For none than he a purer heart could have,
Or that loved good more for itself alone;
Of nought in heaven or earth was he the slave.

PRINCE ATHANASE

What sorrow, strange, and shadowy, and unknown,
Sent him, a hopeless wanderer, through mankind?—
If with a human sadness he did groan,

He had a gentle yet aspiring mind;
Just, innocent, with varied learning fed;
And such a glorious consolation find

In others' joy, when all their own is dead:
He loved, and laboured for his kind in grief,
And yet, unlike all others, it is said

That from such toil he never found relief.
Although a child of fortune and of power,
Of an ancestral name the orphan chief,

His soul had wedded Wisdom, and her dower
Is love and justice, clothed in which he sate
Apart from men, as in a lonely tower,

Pitying the tumult of their dark estate. —
Yet even in youth did he not e'er abuse
The strength of wealth or thought, to consecrate

Those false opinions which the harsh rich use
To blind the world they famish for their pride;
Nor did he hold from any man his dues,

But, like a steward in honest dealings tried,
With those who toiled and wept, the poor and wise,
His riches and his cares he did divide.

PRINCE ATHANASE

Fearless he was, and scorning all disguise,
What he dared do or think, though men might start,
He spoke with mild yet unaverted eyes;

Liberal he was of soul, and frank of heart,
And to his many friends—all loved him well—
Whate'er he knew or felt he would impart,

If words he found those inmost thoughts to tell;
If not, he smiled or wept; and his weak foes
He neither spurned nor hated—though with fell

And mortal hate their thousand voices rose,
They passed like aimless arrows from his ear—
Nor did his heart or mind its portal close

To those, or them, or any, whom life's sphere
May comprehend within its wide array.
What sadness made that vernal spirit sere?—

He knew not. Though his life, day after day,
Was failing like an unreplenished stream,
Though in his eyes a cloud and burthen lay,

Through which his soul, like Vesper's serene beam
Piercing the chasms of ever rising clouds,
Shone, softly burning; though his lips did seem

Like reeds which quiver in impetuous floods;
And through his sleep, and o'er each waking hour,
Thoughts after thoughts, unresting multitudes,

PRINCE ATHANASE

Were driven within him by some secret power,
Which bade them blaze, and live, and roll afar,
Like lights and sounds, from haunted tower to tower

O'er castled mountains borne, when tempest's war
Is levied by the night-contending winds,
And the pale dalesmen watch with eager ear;—

Though such were in his spirit, as the fiends
Which wake and feed an everliving woe,—
What was this grief, which ne'er in other minds

A mirror found,—he knew not—none could know;
But on whoe'er might question him he turned
The light of his frank eyes, as if to show

He knew not of the grief within that burned,
But asked forbearance with a mournful look;
Or spoke in words from which none ever learned

The cause of his disquietude; or shook
With spasms of silent passion; or turned pale:
So that his friends soon rarely undertook

To stir his secret pain without avail;—
For all who knew and loved him then perceived
That there was drawn an adamantine veil

Between his heart and mind,—both unrelieved
Wrought in his brain and bosom separate strife.
Some said that he was mad, others believed

4

PRINCE ATHANASE

That memories of an antenatal life
Made this, where now he dwelt, a penal hell;
And others said that such mysterious grief

From God's displeasure, like a darkness, fell
On souls like his, which owned no higher law
Than love; love calm, steadfast, invincible

By mortal fear or supernatural awe;
And others, — ''Tis the shadow of a dream
Which the veiled eye of Memory never saw,

'But through the soul's abyss, like some dark stream
Through shattered mines and caverns underground,
Rolls, shaking its foundations; and no beam

'Of joy may rise, but it is quenched and drowned
In the dim whirlpools of this dream obscure;
Soon its exhausted waters will have found

'A lair of rest beneath thy spirit pure,
O Athanase!—in one so good and great,
Evil or tumult cannot long endure.'

So spake they: idly of another's state
Babbling vain words and fond philosophy;
This was their consolation; such debate

Men held with one another; nor did he,
Like one who labours with a human woe,
Decline this talk: as if its theme might be

PRINCE ATHANASE

Another, not himself, he to and fro
Questioned and canvassed it with subtlest wit;
And none but those who loved him best could know

That which he knew not, how it galled and bit
His weary mind, this converse vain and cold;
For like an eyeless nightmare grief did sit

Upon his being; a snake which fold by fold
Pressed out the life of life, a clinging fiend
Which clenched him if he stirred with deadlier hold;—
And so his grief remained—let it remain—untold[1].

[1] The Author was pursuing a fuller development of the ideal character of Athanase, when it struck him that in an attempt at extreme refinement and analysis, his conceptions might be betrayed into the assuming a morbid character. The reader will judge whether he is a loser or gainer by this diffidence.

PART II

Fragment 1

PRINCE ATHANASE had one belovèd friend,
An old, old man, with hair of silver white,
And lips where heavenly smiles would hang and blend

With his wise words; and eyes whose arrowy light
Shone like the reflex of a thousand minds.
He was the last whom superstition's blight

Had spared in Greece—the blight that cramps and blinds,—
And in his olive bower at Œnoe
Had sate from earliest youth. Like one who finds

A fertile island in the barren sea,
One mariner who has survived his mates
Many a drear month in a great ship—so he

With soul-sustaining songs, and sweet debates
Of ancient lore, there fed his lonely being:—
'The mind becomes that which it contemplates,'—

And thus Zonoras, by forever seeing
Their bright creations, grew like wisest men;
And when he heard the crash of nations fleeing

A bloodier power than ruled thy ruins then,
O sacred Hellas! many weary years
He wandered, till the path of Laian's glen

7

PRINCE ATHANASE

Was grass-grown—and the unremembered tears
Were dry in Laian for their honoured chief,
Who fell in Byzant, pierced by Moslem spears:—

And as the lady looked with faithful grief
From her high lattice o'er the rugged path,
Where she once saw that horseman toil, with brief

And blighting hope, who with the news of death
Struck body and soul as with a mortal blight,
She saw between the chestnuts, far beneath,

An old man toiling up, a weary wight;
And soon within her hospitable hall
She saw his white hairs glittering in the light

Of the wood fire, and round his shoulders fall;
And his wan visage and his withered mien,
Yet calm and gentle and majestical.

And Athanase, her child, who must have been
Then three years old, sate opposite and gazed
In patient silence.

Fragment 2

SUCH was Zonoras; and as daylight finds
One amaranth glittering on the path of frost,
When autumn nights have nipped all weaker kinds,

PRINCE ATHANASE

Thus through his age, dark, cold, and tempest-tossed,
Shone truth upon Zonoras; and he filled
From fountains pure, nigh overgrown and lost,

The spirit of Prince Athanase, a child,
With soul-sustaining songs of ancient lore
And philosophic wisdom, clear and mild.

And sweet and subtle talk they evermore,
The pupil and the master, shared; until,
Sharing that undiminishable store,

The youth, as shadows on a grassy hill
Outrun the winds that chase them, soon outran
His teacher, and did teach with native skill

Strange truths and new to that experienced man;
Still they were friends, as few have ever been
Who mark the extremes of life's discordant span.

So in the caverns of the forest green,
Or on the rocks of echoing ocean hoar,
Zonoras and Prince Athanase were seen

By summer woodmen; and when winter's roar
Sounded o'er earth and sea its blast of war,
The Balearic fisher, driven from shore,

Hanging upon the peakèd wave afar,
Then saw their lamp from Laian's turret gleam,
Piercing the stormy darkness, like a star

PRINCE ATHANASE

Which pours beyond the sea one steadfast beam,
Whilst all the constellations of the sky
Seemed reeling through the storm . . . They did but seem —

For, lo! the wintry clouds are all gone by,
And bright Arcturus through yon pines is glowing,
And far o'er southern waves, immovably

Belted Orion hangs — warm light is flowing
From the young moon into the sunset's chasm. —
'O, summer eve! with power divine, bestowing

'On thine own bird the sweet enthusiasm
Which overflows in notes of liquid gladness,
Filling the sky like light! How many a spasm

'Of fevered brains, oppressed with grief and madness,
Were lulled by thee, delightful nightingale, —
And these soft waves, murmuring a gentle sadness, —

'And the far sighings of yon piny dale
Made vocal by some wind we feel not here. —
I bear alone what nothing may avail

'To lighten — a strange load!' — No human ear
Heard this lament; but o'er the visage wan
Of Athanase, a ruffling atmosphere

Of dark emotion, a swift shadow, ran,
Like wind upon some forest-bosomed lake,
Glassy and dark. — And that divine old man

PRINCE ATHANASE

Beheld his mystic friend's whole being shake,
Even where its inmost depths were gloomiest—
And with a calm and measured voice he spake,

And, with a soft and equal pressure, pressed
That cold lean hand:—'Dost thou remember yet
When the curved moon then lingering in the west

'Paused, in yon waves her mighty horns to wet,
How in those beams we walked, half resting on the sea?
'Tis just one year—sure thou dost not forget—

'Then Plato's words of light in thee and me
Lingered like moonlight in the moonless east,
For we had just then read—thy memory

'Is faithful now—the story of the feast;
And Agathon and Diotima seemed
From death and dark forgetfulness released . . . . .'

Fragment 3

AND when the old man saw that on the green
Leaves of his opening   a blight had lighted
He said: 'My friend, one grief alone can wean

A gentle mind from all that once delighted:—
Thou lovest, and thy secret heart is laden
With feelings which should not be unrequited.'

PRINCE ATHANASE

And Athanase . . . then smiled, as one o'erladen
With iron chains might smile to talk (?) of bands
Twined round her lover's neck by some blithe maiden,
And said . . . . .

Fragment 4

'TWAS at the season when the Earth upsprings
From slumber, as a spherèd angel's child,
Shadowing its eyes with green and golden wings,

Stands up before its mother bright and mild,
Of whose soft voice the air expectant seems—
So stood before the sun, which shone and smiled

To see it rise thus joyous from its dreams,
The fresh and radiant Earth. The hoary grove
Waxed green—and flowers burst forth like starry beams;—

The grass in the warm sun did start and move,
And sea-buds burst under the waves serene:—
How many a one, though none be near to love,

Loves then the shade of his own soul, half seen
In any mirror—or the spring's young minions,
The wingèd leaves amid the corpses green;—

How many a spirit then puts on the pinions
Of fancy, and outstrips the lagging blast,
And his own steps—and over wide dominions

PRINCE ATHANASE

Sweeps in his dream-drawn chariot, far and fast,
More fleet than storms—the wide world shrinks below,
When winter and despondency are past.

Fragment 5.

'TWAS at this season that Prince Athanase
Passed the white Alps—those eagle-baffling mountains
Slept in their shrouds of snow;—beside the ways

The waterfalls were voiceless—for their fountains
Were changed to mines of sunless crystal now,
Or by the curdling winds—like brazen wings

Which clanged along the mountain's marble brow—
Warped into adamantine fretwork, hung
And filled with frozen light the chasms below.

Vexed by the blast, the great pines groaned and swung
Under their load of [snow]— .   .   .
        .   .   .   .   .
        .   .   .   .   .

Such as the eagle sees, when he dives down
From the gray deserts of wide air, [beheld]
[Prince] Athanase; and o'er his mien (?) was thrown

The shadow of that scene, field after field,
Purple and dim and wide . . . . .

PRINCE ATHANASE

Fragment 6

THOU art the wine whose drunkenness is all
We can desire, O Love! and happy souls,
Ere from thy vine the leaves of autumn fall,

Catch thee, and feed from their o'erflowing bowls
Thousands who thirst for thine ambrosial dew;—
Thou art the radiance which where ocean rolls

Investeth it; and when the heavens are blue
Thou fillest them; and when the earth is fair
The shadow of thy moving wings imbue

Its deserts and its mountains, till they wear
Beauty like some light robe; thou ever soarest
Among the towers of men, and as soft air

In spring, which moves the unawakened forest,
Clothing with leaves its branches bare and bleak,
Thou floatest among men; and aye implorest

That which from thee they should implore: the weak
Alone kneel to thee, offering up the hearts
The strong have broken—yet where shall any seek

A garment whom thou clothest not? the darts
Of the keen winter storm, barbèd with frost,
Which, from the everlasting snow that parts

PRINCE ATHANASE

The Alps from Heaven, pierce some traveller lost
In the wide waved interminable snow
Ungarmented, ...

Another Fragment (a)

YES, often when the eyes are cold and dry,
And the lips calm, the Spirit weeps within
Tears bitterer than the blood of agony

Trembling in drops on the discoloured skin
Of those who love their kind and therefore perish
In ghastly torture—a sweet medicine

Of peace and sleep are tears, and quietly
Them soothe from whose uplifted eyes they fall
But . . . . .

Another Fragment (b)

HER hair was brown, her spherèd eyes were brown,
And in their dark and liquid moisture swam,
Like the dim orb of the eclipsèd moon;

Yet when the spirit flashed beneath, there came
The light from them, as when tears of delight
Double the western planet's serene flame.

1817.

15

ROSALIND AND HELEN

A

MODERN ECLOGUE

*

ADVERTISEMENT

THE story of *Rosalind and Helen* is, undoubtedly, not an attempt in the highest style of poetry. It is in no degree calculated to excite profound meditation; and if, by interesting the affections and amusing the imagination, it awakens a certain ideal melancholy favourable to the reception of more important impressions, it will produce in the reader all that the writer experienced in the composition. I resigned myself, as I wrote, to the impulse of the feelings which moulded the conception of the story; and this impulse determined the pauses of a measure, which only pretends to be regular inasmuch as it corresponds with, and expresses, the irregularity of the imaginations which inspired it.

I do not know which of the few scattered poems I left in England will be selected by my bookseller to add to this collection. One, which I sent from Italy, was written after a day's excursion among those lovely mountains which surround what was once the retreat, and where is now the sepulchre, of Petrarch. If any one is inclined

ROSALIND AND HELEN

to condemn the insertion of the introductory lines,
which image forth the sudden relief of a state of deep
despondency by the radiant visions disclosed by the
sudden burst of an Italian sunrise in autumn on the
highest peak of those delightful mountains, I can only
offer as my excuse, that they were not erased at the
request of a dear friend, with whom added years of
intercourse only add to my apprehension of its value,
and who would have had more right than any one to
complain, that she has not been able to extinguish in
me the very power of delineating sadness.

Naples, *Dec.* 20, 1818.

ROSALIND, HELEN & HER CHILD

Scene, the Shore of the Lake of Como

HELEN. Come hither, my sweet Rosalind.
'Tis long since thou and I have met;
And yet methinks it were unkind
Those moments to forget.
Come sit by me. I see thee stand
By this lone lake, in this far land,
Thy loose hair in the light wind flying,
Thy sweet voice to each tone of even
United, and thine eyes replying
To the hues of yon fair heaven.
Come, gentle friend: wilt sit by me?
And be as thou wert wont to be
Ere we were disunited?
None doth behold us now: the power
That led us forth at this lone hour
Will be but ill requited
If thou depart in scorn: oh! come,
And talk of our abandoned home.
Remember, this is Italy,
And we are exiles. Talk with me
Of that our land, whose wilds and floods,
Barren and dark although they be,

ROSALIND AND HELEN

Were dearer than these chestnut woods:
Those heathy paths, that inland stream,
And the blue mountains, shapes which seem
Like wrecks of childhood's sunny dream:
Which that we have abandoned now,
Weighs on the heart like that remorse
Which altered friendship leaves. I seek
No more our youthful intercourse.
That cannot be! Rosalind, speak.
Speak to me. Leave me not. — When morn did come,
When evening fell upon our common home,
When for one hour we parted, — do not frown:
I would not chide thee, though thy faith is broken:
But turn to me. Oh! by this cherished token,
Of woven hair, which thou wilt not disown,
Turn, as 'twere but the memory of me,
And not my scornèd self who prayed to thee.
    ROSALIND. Is it a dream, or do I see
And hear frail Helen? I would flee
Thy tainting touch; but former years
Arise, and bring forbidden tears;
And my o'erburthened memory
Seeks yet its lost repose in thee.
I share thy crime. I cannot choose
But weep for thee: mine own strange grief
But seldom stoops to such relief:

ROSALIND AND HELEN

Nor ever did I love thee less,
Though mourning o'er thy wickedness
Even with a sister's woe. I knew
What to the evil world is due,
And therefore sternly did refuse
To link me with the infamy
Of one so lost as Helen. Now
Bewildered by my dire despair,
Wondering I blush, and weep that thou
Should'st love me still,—thou only!—There,
Let us sit on that gray stone,
Till our mournful talk be done.

    HELEN. Alas! not there; I cannot bear
The murmur of this lake to hear.
A sound from there, Rosalind dear,
Which never yet I heard elsewhere
But in our native land, recurs,
Even here where now we meet. It stirs
Too much of suffocating sorrow!
In the dell of yon dark chestnut wood
Is a stone seat, a solitude
Less like our own. The ghost of Peace
Will not desert this spot. To-morrow,
If thy kind feelings should not cease,
We may sit here.

    ROSALIND. Thou lead, my sweet,

ROSALIND AND HELEN

And I will follow.

    HENRY.   'Tis Fenici's seat
Where you are going? This is not the way,
Mamma; it leads behind those trees that grow
Close to the little river.

    HELEN.   Yes: I know:
I was bewildered. Kiss me, and be gay,
Dear boy: why do you sob?

    HENRY.   I do not know:
But it might break any one's heart to see
You and the lady cry so bitterly.

    HELEN. It is a gentle child, my friend. Go home,
Henry, and play with Lilla till I come.
We only cried with joy to see each other:
We are quite merry now: Good-night.

                      The boy
Lifted a sudden look upon his mother,
And in the gleam of forced and hollow joy
Which lightened o'er her face, laughed with the glee
Of light and unsuspecting infancy,
And whispered in her ear, 'Bring home with you
That sweet strange lady-friend.' Then off he flew,
But stopped, and beckoned with a meaning smile,
Where the road turned. Pale Rosalind the while,
Hiding her face, stood weeping silently.

ROSALIND AND HELEN

In silence then they took the way
Beneath the forest's solitude.
It was a vast and antique wood,
Thro' which they took their way;
And the gray shades of evening
O'er that green wilderness did fling
Still deeper solitude.
Pursuing still the path that wound
The vast and knotted trees around
Through which slow shades were wandering,
To a deep lawny dell they came,
To a stone seat beside a spring,
O'er which the columned wood did frame
A roofless temple, like the fane
Where, ere new creeds could faith obtain,
Man's early race once knelt beneath
The overhanging deity.
O'er this fair fountain hung the sky,
Now spangled with rare stars. The snake,
The pale snake, that with eager breath
Creeps here his noontide thirst to slake,
Is beaming with many a mingled hue,
Shed from yon dome's eternal blue,
When he floats on that dark and lucid flood
In the light of his own loveliness;
And the birds that in the fountain dip

22

ROSALIND AND HELEN

Their plumes, with fearless fellowship
Above and round him wheel and hover.
The fitful wind is heard to stir
One solitary leaf on high;
The chirping of the grasshopper
Fills every pause. There is emotion
In all that dwells at noontide here:
Then, through the intricate wild wood,
A maze of life and light and motion
Is woven. But there is stillness now:
Gloom, and the trance of Nature now:
The snake is in his cave asleep;
The birds are on the branches dreaming:
Only the shadows creep:
Only the glow-worm is gleaming:
Only the owls and the nightingales
Wake in this dell when daylight fails,
And gray shades gather in the woods:
And the owls have all fled far away
In a merrier glen to hoot and play,
For the moon is veiled and sleeping now.
The accustomed nightingale still broods
On her accustomed bough,
But she is mute; for her false mate
Has fled and left her desolate.

ROSALIND AND HELEN

This silent spot tradition old
Had peopled with the spectral dead.
For the roots of the speaker's hair felt cold
And stiff, as with tremulous lips he told
That a hellish shape at midnight led
The ghost of a youth with hoary hair,
And sate on the seat beside him there,
Till a naked child came wandering by,
When the fiend would change to a lady fair !
A fearful tale ! The truth was worse:
For here a sister and a brother
Had solemnized a monstrous curse,
Meeting in this fair solitude:
For beneath yon very sky,
Had they resigned to one another
Body and soul. The multitude:
Tracking them to the secret wood,
Tore limb from limb their innocent child,
And stabbed and trampled on its mother;
But the youth, for God's most holy grace,
A priest saved to burn in the market-place.

Duly at evening Helen came
To this lone silent spot,
From the wrecks of a tale of wilder sorrow
So much of sympathy to borrow

24

ROSALIND AND HELEN

As soothed her own dark lot.
Duly each evening from her home,
With her fair child would Helen come
To sit upon that antique seat,
While the hues of day were pale;
And the bright boy beside her feet
Now lay, lifting at intervals
His broad blue eyes on her;
Now, where some sudden impulse calls
Following. He was a gentle boy
And in all gentle sports took joy;
Oft in a dry leaf for a boat,
With a small feather for a sail,
His fancy on that spring would float,
If some invisible breeze might stir
Its marble calm: and Helen smiled
Through tears of awe on the gay child,
To think that a boy as fair as he,
In years which never more may be,
By that same fount, in that same wood,
The like sweet fancies had pursued;
And that a mother, lost like her,
Had mournfully sate watching him.
Then all the scene was wont to swim
Through the mist of a burning tear.

ROSALIND AND HELEN

For many months had Helen known
This scene; and now she thither turned
Her footsteps, not alone.
The friend whose falsehood she had mourned,
Sate with her on that seat of stone.
Silent they sate; for evening,
And the power its glimpses bring
Had, with one awful shadow, quelled
The passion of their grief. They sate
With linkèd hands, for unrepelled
Had Helen taken Rosalind's.
Like the autumn wind, when it unbinds
The tangled locks of the nightshade's hair,
Which is twined in the sultry summer air
Round the walls of an outworn sepulchre,
Did the voice of Helen, sad and sweet,
And the sound of her heart that ever beat,
As with sighs and words she breathed on her,
Unbind the knots of her friend's despair,
Till her thoughts were free to float and flow;
And from her labouring bosom now,
Like the bursting of a prisoned flame,
The voice of a long pent sorrow came.
    ROSALIND. I saw the dark earth fall upon
The coffin; and I saw the stone
Laid over him whom this cold breast

ROSALIND AND HELEN

Had pillowed to his nightly rest!
Thou knowest not, thou canst not know
My agony. Oh! I could not weep:
The sources whence such blessings flow
Were not to be approached by me!
But I could smile, and I could sleep,
Though with a self-accusing heart.
In morning's light, in evening's gloom,
I watched, —and would not thence depart—
My husband's unlamented tomb.
My children knew their sire was gone,
But when I told them, —'he is dead,'—
They laughed aloud in frantic glee,
They clapped their hands and leaped about,
Answering each other's ecstasy
With many a prank and merry shout.
But I sate silent and alone,
Wrapped in the mock of mourning weed.

They laughed, for he was dead: but I
Sate with a hard and tearless eye,
And with a heart which would deny
The secret joy it could not quell,
Low muttering o'er his loathèd name;
Till from that self-contention came
Remorse where sin was none; a hell

ROSALIND AND HELEN

Which in pure spirits should not dwell.
I'll tell thee truth. He was a man
Hard, selfish, loving only gold,
Yet full of guile: his pale eyes ran
With tears, which each some falsehood told,
And oft his smooth and bridled tongue
Would give the lie to his flushing cheek:
He was a coward to the strong:
He was a tyrant to the weak,
On whom his vengeance he would wreak:
For scorn, whose arrows search the heart,
From many a stranger's eye would dart,
And on his memory cling, and follow
His soul to its home so cold and hollow.
He was a tyrant to the weak,
And we were such, alas the day!
Oft, when my little ones at play,
Were in youth's natural lightness gay,
Or if they listened to some tale
Of travellers, or of fairy land, —
When the light from the wood-fire's dying brand
Flashed on their faces, —if they heard
Or thought they heard upon the stair
His footstep, the suspended word
Died on my lips: we all grew pale:
The babe at my bosom was hushed with fear

ROSALIND AND HELEN

If it thought it heard its father near;
And my two wild boys would near my knee
Cling, cowed and cowering fearfully.

I'll tell thee truth: I loved another.
His name in my ear was ever ringing,
His form to my brain was ever clinging:
Yet if some stranger breathed that name,
My lips turned white, and my heart beat fast:
My nights were once haunted by dreams of flame,
My days were dim in the shadow cast
By the memory of the same!
Day and night, day and night,
He was my breath and life and light,
For three short years, which soon were passed.
On the fourth, my gentle mother
Led me to the shrine, to be
His sworn bride eternally.
And now we stood on the altar stair,
When my father came from a distant land,
And with a loud and fearful cry
Rushed between us suddenly.
I saw the stream of his thin gray hair,
I saw his lean and lifted hand,
And heard his words, —and live! Oh God!
Wherefore do I live?—'Hold, hold!'

ROSALIND AND HELEN

He cried, — 'I tell thee 'tis her brother!
Thy mother, boy, beneath the sod
Of yon churchyard rests in her shroud so cold:
I am now weak, and pale, and old:
We were once dear to one another,
I and that corpse! Thou art our child!'
Then with a laugh both long and wild
The youth upon the pavement fell:
They found him dead! All looked on me,
The spasms of my despair to see:
But I was calm. I went away:
I was clammy-cold like clay!
I did not weep: I did not speak:
But day by day, week after week,
I walked about like a corpse alive!
Alas! sweet friend, you must believe
This heart is stone: it did not break.
My father lived a little while,
But all might see that he was dying,
He smiled with such a woeful smile!
When he was in the churchyard lying
Among the worms, we grew quite poor,
So that no one would give us bread:
My mother looked at me, and said
Faint words of cheer, which only meant
That she could die and be content;

ROSALIND AND HELEN

So I went forth from the same church door
To another husband's bed.
And this was he who died at last,
When weeks and months and years had passed,
Through which I firmly did fulfil
My duties, a devoted wife,
With the stern step of vanquished will,
Walking beneath the night of life,
Whose hours extinguished, like slow rain
Falling for ever, pain by pain,
The very hope of death's dear rest;
Which, since the heart within my breast
Of natural life was dispossessed,
Its strange sustainer there had been.

When flowers were dead, and grass was green
Upon my mother's grave, —that mother
Whom to outlive, and cheer, and make
My wan eyes glitter for her sake,
Was my vowed task, the single care
Which once gave life to my despair, —
When she was a thing that did not stir
And the crawling worms were cradling her
To a sleep more deep and so more sweet
Than a baby's rocked on its nurse's knee,
I lived: a living pulse then beat

ROSALIND AND HELEN

Beneath my heart that awakened me.
What was this pulse so warm and free?
Alas! I knew it could not be
My own dull blood: 'twas like a thought
Of liquid love, that spread and wrought
Under my bosom and in my brain,
And crept with the blood through every vein;
And hour by hour, day after day,
The wonder could not charm away,
But laid in sleep, my wakeful pain,
Until I knew it was a child,
And then I wept. For long, long years
These frozen eyes had shed no tears:
But now — 'twas the season fair and mild
When April has wept itself to May:
I sate through the sweet sunny day
By my window bowered round with leaves,
And down my cheeks the quick tears fell
Like twinkling rain-drops from the eaves,
When warm spring showers are passing o'er:
O Helen, none can ever tell
The joy it was to weep once more!

I wept to think how hard it were
To kill my babe, and take from it
The sense of light, and the warm air,

ROSALIND AND HELEN

And my own fond and tender care,
And love and smiles; ere I knew yet
That these for it might, as for me,
Be the masks of a grinning mockery.
And haply, I would dream, 'twere sweet
To feed it from my faded breast,
Or mark my own heart's restless beat
Rock it to its untroubled rest,
And watch the growing soul beneath
Dawn in faint smiles; and hear its breath,
Half interrupted by calm sighs,
And search the depth of its fair eyes
For long departed memories!
And so I lived till that sweet load
Was lightened. Darkly forward flowed
The stream of years, and on it bore
Two shapes of gladness to my sight;
Two other babes, delightful more
In my lost soul's abandoned night,
Than their own country ships may be
Sailing towards wrecked mariners,
Who cling to the rock of a wintry sea.
For each, as it came, brought soothing tears,
And a loosening warmth, as each one lay
Sucking the sullen milk away
About my frozen heart, did play,

ROSALIND AND HELEN

And weaned it, oh how painfully!—
As they themselves were weaned each one
From that sweet food,—even from the thirst
Of death, and nothingness, and rest,
Strange inmate of a living breast!
Which all that I had undergone
Of grief and shame, since she, who first
The gates of that dark refuge closed,
Came to my sight, and almost burst
The seal of that Lethean spring;
But these fair shadows interposed:
For all delights are shadows now!
And from my brain to my dull brow
The heavy tears gather and flow:
I cannot speak: Oh let me weep!

The tears which fell from her wan eyes
Glimmered among the moonlight dew:
Her deep hard sobs and heavy sighs
Their echoes in the darkness threw.
When she grew calm, she thus did keep
The tenor of her tale:
                        He died:
I know not how: he was not old,
If age be numbered by its years:
But he was bowed and bent with fears,

ROSALIND AND HELEN

Pale with the quenchless thirst of gold,
Which, like fierce fever, left him weak;
And his strait lip and bloated cheek
Were warped in spasms by hollow sneers;
And selfish cares with barren plough,
Not age, had lined his narrow brow,
And foul and cruel thoughts, which feed
Upon the withering life within,
Like vipers on some poisonous weed.
Whether his ill were death or sin
None knew, until he died indeed,
And then men owned they were the same.

Seven days within my chamber lay
That corse, and my babes made holiday:
At last, I told them what is death:
The eldest, with a kind of shame,
Came to my knees with silent breath,
And sate awe-stricken at my feet;
And soon the others left their play,
And sate there too. It is unmeet
To shed on the brief flower of youth
The withering knowledge of the grave;
From me remorse then wrung that truth.
I could not bear the joy which gave
Too just a response to mine own.

ROSALIND AND HELEN

In vain. I dared not feign a groan,
And in their artless looks I saw,
Between the mists of fear and awe,
That my own thought was theirs, and they
Expressed it not in words, but said,
Each in its heart, how every day
Will pass in happy work and play,
Now he is dead and gone away.

After the funeral all our kin
Assembled, and the will was read.
My friend, I tell thee, even the dead
Have strength, their putrid shrouds within,
To blast and torture. Those who live
Still fear the living, but a corse
Is merciless, and power doth give
To such pale tyrants half the spoil
He rends from those who groan and toil,
Because they blush not with remorse
Among their crawling worms. Behold,
I have no child! my tale grows old
With grief, and staggers: let it reach
The limits of my feeble speech,
And languidly at length recline
On the brink of its own grave and mine.

ROSALIND AND HELEN

Thou knowest what a thing is Poverty
Among the fallen on evil days:
'Tis Crime, and Fear, and Infamy,
And houseless Want in frozen ways
Wandering ungarmented, and Pain,
And, worse than all, that inward stain
Foul Self-contempt, which drowns in sneers
Youth's starlight smile, and makes its tears
First like hot gall, then dry for ever!
And well thou knowest a mother never
Could doom her children to this ill,
And well he knew the same. The will
Imported, that if e'er again
I sought my children to behold,
Or in my birthplace did remain
Beyond three days, whose hours were told,
They should inherit nought: and he,
To whom next came their patrimony,
A sallow lawyer, cruel and cold,
Aye watched me, as the will was read,
With eyes askance, which sought to see
The secrets of my agony;
And with close lips and anxious brow
Stood canvassing still to and fro
The chance of my resolve, and all
The dead man's caution just did call;

ROSALIND AND HELEN

For in that killing lie 'twas said—
' She is adulterous, and doth hold
In secret that the Christian creed
Is false, and therefore is much need
That I should have a care to save
My children from eternal fire.'
Friend, he was sheltered by the grave,
And therefore dared to be a liar!
In truth, the Indian on the pyre
Of her dead husband, half consumed,
As well might there be false, as I
To those abhorred embraces doomed,
Far worse than fire's brief agony
As to the Christian creed, if true
Or false, I never questioned it:
I took it as the vulgar do:
Nor my vexed soul had leisure yet
To doubt the things men say, or deem
That they are other than they seem.

All present who those crimes did hear,
In feigned or actual scorn and fear,
Men, women, children, slunk away,
Whispering with self-contented pride,
Which half suspects its own base lie.
I spoke to none, nor did abide,

ROSALIND AND HELEN

But silently I went my way,
Nor noticed I where joyously
Sate my two younger babes at play,
In the court-yard through which I passed;
But went with footsteps firm and fast
Till I came to the brink of the ocean green,
And there, a woman with gray hairs,
Who had my mother's servant been,
Kneeling, with many tears and prayers,
Made me accept a purse of gold,
Half of the earnings she had kept
To refuge her when weak and old.

With woe, which never sleeps or slept,
I wander now. 'Tis a vain thought —
But on yon alp, whose snowy head
'Mid the azure air is islanded,
(We see it o'er the flood of cloud,
Which sunrise from its eastern caves
Drives, wrinkling into golden waves,
Hung with its precipices proud,
From that gray stone where first we met)
There now — who knows the dead feel nought? —
Should be my grave; for he who yet
Is my soul's soul, once said: ''Twere sweet
'Mid stars and lightnings to abide,

ROSALIND AND HELEN

And winds and lulling snows, that beat
With their soft flakes the mountain wide,
Where weary meteor lamps repose,
And languid storms their pinions close;
And all things strong and bright and pure,
And ever during, aye endure:
Who knows, if one were buried there,
But these things might our spirits make,
Amid the all-surrounding air,
Their own eternity partake?'
Then 'twas a wild and playful saying
At which I laughed, or seemed to laugh:
They were his words: now heed my praying,
And let them be my epitaph.
Thy memory for a term may be
My monument. Wilt remember me?
I know thou wilt, and canst forgive
Whilst in this erring world to live
My soul disdained not, that I thought
Its lying forms were worthy aught
And much less thee.
  HELEN.   O speak not so,
But come to me and pour thy woe
Into this heart, full though it be,
Ay, overflowing with its own:
I thought that grief had severed me

ROSALIND AND HELEN

From all beside who weep and groan;
Its likeness upon earth to be,
Its express image; but thou art
More wretched. Sweet! we will not part
Henceforth, if death be not division;
If so, the dead feel no contrition.
But wilt thou hear since last we parted
All that has left me broken hearted?

    ROSALIND. Yes, speak. The faintest stars are
        scarcely shorn
Of their thin beams by that delusive morn
Which sinks again in darkness, like the light
Of early love, soon lost in total night.

    HELEN. Alas! Italian winds are mild,
But my bosom is cold—wintry cold—
When the warm air weaves, among the fresh leaves,
Soft music, my poor brain is wild,
And I am weak like a nursling child,
Though my soul with grief is gray and old.

    ROSALIND. Weep not at thine own words, though
        they must make
Me weep. What is thy tale?

    HELEN.   I fear 'twill shake
Thy gentle heart with tears. Thou well
Rememberest when we met no more,
And, though I dwelt with Lionel,

ROSALIND AND HELEN

That friendless caution pierced me sore
With grief; a wound my spirit bore
Indignantly, but when he died
With him lay dead both hope and pride.
Alas! all hope is buried now.
But then men dreamed the agèd earth
Was labouring in that mighty birth,
Which many a poet and a sage
Has aye foreseen—the happy age
When truth and love shall dwell below
Among the works and ways of men;
Which on this world not power but will
Even now is wanting to fulfil.

Among mankind what thence befell
Of strife, how vain, is known too well;
When Liberty's dear paean fell
'Mid murderous howls. To Lionel,
Though of great wealth and lineage high,
Yet through those dungeon walls there came
Thy thrilling light, O Liberty!
And as the meteor's midnight flame
Startles the dreamer, sun-like truth
Flashed on his visionary youth,
And filled him, not with love, but faith,
And hope, and courage mute in death;

ROSALIND AND HELEN

For love and life in him were twins,
Born at one birth: in every other
First life then love its course begins,
Though they be children of one mother;
And so through this dark world they fleet
Divided, till in death they meet:
But he loved all things ever. Then
He passed amid the strife of men,
And stood at the throne of armèd power
Pleading for a world of woe:
Secure as one on a rock-built tower
O'er the wrecks which the surge trails to and fro,
'Mid the passions wild of human kind
He stood, like a spirit calming them;
For, it was said, his words could bind
Like music the lulled crowd, and stem
That torrent of unquiet dream,
Which mortals truth and reason deem,
But is revenge and fear and pride.
Joyous he was; and hope and peace
On all who heard him did abide,
Raining like dew from his sweet talk,
As where the evening star may walk
Along the brink of the gloomy seas,
Liquid mists of splendour quiver.
His very gestures touched to tears

ROSALIND AND HELEN

The unpersuaded tyrant, never
So moved before: his presence stung
The torturers with their victim's pain,
And none knew how; and through their ears,
The subtle witchcraft of his tongue
Unlocked the hearts of those who keep
Gold, the world's bond of slavery.
Men wondered, and some sneered to see
One sow what he could never reap:
For he is rich, they said, and young,
And might drink from the depths of luxury.
If he seeks Fame, Fame never crowned
The champion of a trampled creed:
If he seeks Power, Power is enthroned
'Mid ancient rights and wrongs, to feed
Which hungry wolves with praise and spoil,
Those who would sit near Power must toil;
And such, there sitting, all may see.
What seeks he? All that others seek
He casts away, like a vile weed
Which the sea casts unreturningly.
That poor and hungry men should break
The laws which wreak them toil and scorn,
We understand; but Lionel
We know is rich and nobly born.
So wondered they: yet all men loved

ROSALIND AND HELEN

Young Lionel, though few approved;
All but the priests, whose hatred fell
Like the unseen blight of a smiling day,
The withering honey dew, which clings
Under the bright green buds of May,
Whilst they unfold their emerald wings:
For he made verses wild and queer
On the strange creeds priests hold so dear,
Because they bring them land and gold.
Of devils and saints and all such gear,
He made tales which whoso heard or read
Would laugh till he were almost dead.
So this grew a proverb: 'Don't get old
Till Lionel's "Banquet in Hell" you hear,
And then you will laugh yourself young again.'
So the priests hated him, and he
Repaid their hate with cheerful glee.

Ah, smiles and joyance quickly died,
For public hope grew pale and dim
In an altered time and tide,
And in its wasting withered him,
As a summer flower that blows too soon
Droops in the smile of the waning moon,
When it scatters through an April night
The frozen dews of wrinkling blight.

ROSALIND AND HELEN

None now hoped more. Gray Power was seated
Safely on her ancestral throne;
And Faith, the Python, undefeated,
Even to its blood-stained steps dragged on
Her foul and wounded train, and men
Were trampled and deceived again,
And words and shows again could bind
The wailing tribes of human kind
In scorn and famine. Fire and blood
Raged round the raging multitude,
To fields remote by tyrants sent
To be the scornèd instrument
With which they drag from mines of gore
The chains their slaves yet ever wore:
And in the streets men met each other,
And by old altars and in halls,
And smiled again at festivals.
But each man found in his heart's brother
Cold cheer; for all, though half deceived,
The outworn creeds again believed,
And the same round anew began,
Which the weary world yet ever ran.

Many then wept, not tears, but gall
Within their hearts, like drops which fall
Wasting the fountain-stone away.

ROSALIND AND HELEN

And in that dark and evil day
Did all desires and thoughts, that claim
Men's care—ambition, friendship, fame,
Love, hope, though hope was now despair—
Indue the colours of this change,
As from the all-surrounding air
The earth takes hues obscure and strange,
When storm and earthquake linger there.

And so, my friend, it then befell
To many, most to Lionel,
Whose hope was like the life of youth
Within him, and when dead, became
A spirit of unresting flame,
Which goaded him in his distress
Over the world's vast wilderness.
Three years he left his native land,
And on the fourth, when he returned,
None knew him: he was stricken deep
With some disease of mind, and turned
Into aught unlike Lionel.
On him, on whom, did he pause in sleep,
Serenest smiles were wont to keep,
And, did he wake, a wingèd band
Of bright persuasions, which had fed
On his sweet lips and liquid eyes,

ROSALIND AND HELEN

Kept their swift pinions half outspread,
To do on men his least command;
On him, whom once 'twas paradise
Even to behold, now misery lay:
In his own heart 'twas merciless,
To all things else none may express
Its innocence and tenderness.

'Twas said that he had refuge sought
In love from his unquiet thought
In distant lands, and been deceived
By some strange show; for there were found,
Blotted with tears as those relieved
By their own words are wont to do,
These mournful verses on the ground,
By all who read them blotted too.

'How am I changed! my hopes were once like fire:
I loved, and I believed that life was love.
How am I lost! on wings of swift desire
Among Heaven's winds my spirit once did move.
I slept, and silver dreams did aye inspire
My liquid sleep: I woke, and did approve
All nature to my heart, and thought to make
A paradise of earth for one sweet sake.

ROSALIND AND HELEN

'I love, but I believe in love no more.
I feel desire, but hope not. O, from sleep
Most vainly must my weary brain implore
Its long lost flattery now: I wake to weep,
And sit through the long day gnawing the core
Of my bitter heart, and, like a miser, keep,
Since none in what I feel take pain or pleasure,
To my own soul its self-consuming treasure.'

He dwelt beside me near the sea:
And oft in evening did we meet,
When the waves, beneath the starlight, flee
O'er the yellow sands with silver feet,
And talked: our talk was sad and sweet,
Till slowly from his mien there passed
The desolation which it spoke;
And smiles, — as when the lightning's blast
Has parched some heaven-delighting oak,
The next spring shows leaves pale and rare,
But like flowers delicate and fair,
On its rent boughs, — again arrayed
His countenance in tender light:
His words grew subtile fire, which made
The air his hearers breathed delight:
His motions, like the winds, were free,
Which bend the bright grass gracefully,

ROSALIND AND HELEN

Then fade away in circlets faint:
And wingèd Hope, on which upborne
His soul seemed hovering in his eyes,
Like some bright spirit newly born
Floating amid the sunny skies,
Sprang forth from his rent heart anew.
Yet o'er his talk, and looks, and mien,
Tempering their loveliness too keen,
Past woe its shadow backward threw,
Till like an exhalation, spread
From flowers half drunk with evening dew,
They did become infectious: sweet
And subtile mists of sense and thought:
Which wrapped us soon, when we might meet,
Almost from our own looks and aught
The wide world holds. And so, his mind
Was healed, while mine grew sick with fear:
For ever now his health declined,
Like some frail bark which cannot bear
The impulse of an altered wind,
Though prosperous: and my heart grew full
'Mid its new joy of a new care:
For his cheek became, not pale, but fair,
As rose-o'ershadowed lilies are;
And soon his deep and sunny hair,
In this alone less beautiful,

ROSALIND AND HELEN

Like grass in tombs grew wild and rare.
The blood in his translucent veins
Beat, not like animal life, but love
Seemed now its sullen springs to move,
When life had failed, and all its pains:
And sudden sleep would seize him oft
Like death, so calm, but that a tear,
His pointed eyelashes between,
Would gather in the light serene
Of smiles, whose lustre bright and soft
Beneath lay undulating there.
His breath was like inconstant flame,
As eagerly it went and came;
And I hung o'er him in his sleep,
Till, like an image in the lake
Which rains disturb, my tears would break
The shadow of that slumber deep:
Then he would bid me not to weep,
And say with flattery false, yet sweet,
That death and he could never meet,
If I would never part with him.
And so we loved, and did unite
All that in us was yet divided:
For when he said, that many a rite,
By men to bind but once provided,
Could not be shared by him and me,

ROSALIND AND HELEN

Or they would kill him in their glee,
I shuddered, and then laughing said—
'We will have rites our faith to bind,
But our church shall be the starry night,
Our altar the grassy earth outspread,
And our priest the muttering wind.'

'Twas sunset as I spoke: one star
Had scarce burst forth, when from afar
The ministers of misrule sent,
Seized upon Lionel, and bore
His chained limbs to a dreary tower,
In the midst of a city vast and wide.
For he, they said, from his mind had bent
Against their gods keen blasphemy,
For which, though his soul must roasted be
In hell's red lakes immortally,
Yet even on earth must he abide
The vengeance of their slaves: a trial,
I think, men call it. What avail
Are prayers and tears, which chase denial
From the fierce savage, nursed in hate?
What the knit soul that pleading and pale
Makes wan the quivering cheek, which late
It painted with its own delight?
We were divided. As I could,

ROSALIND AND HELEN

I stilled the tingling of my blood,
And followed him in their despite,
As a widow follows, pale and wild,
The murderers and corse of her only child;
And when we came to the prison door
And I prayed to share his dungeon floor
With prayers which rarely have been spurned,
And when men drove me forth and I
Stared with blank frenzy on the sky,
A farewell look of love he turned,
Half calming me; then gazed awhile,
As if thro' that black and massy pile,
And thro' the crowd around him there,
And thro' the dense and murky air,
And the thronged streets, he did espy
What poets know and prophesy;
And said, with voice that made them shiver
And clung like music in my brain,
And which the mute walls spoke again
Prolonging it with deepened strain:
'Fear not the tyrants shall rule for ever,
Or the priests of the bloody faith;
They stand on the brink of that mighty river,
Whose waves they have tainted with death:
It is fed from the depths of a thousand dells,
Around them it foams, and rages, and swells,

ROSALIND AND HELEN

And their swords and their sceptres I floating see,
Like wrecks in the surge of eternity.'

I dwelt beside the prison gate,
And the strange crowd that out and in
Passed, some, no doubt, with mine own fate,
Might have fretted me with its ceaseless din,
But the fever of care was louder within.
Soon, but too late, in penitence
Or fear, his foes released him thence:
I saw his thin and languid form,
As leaning on the jailor's arm,
Whose hardened eyes grew moist the while,
To meet his mute and faded smile,
And hear his words of kind farewell,
He tottered forth from his damp cell.
Many had never wept before,
From whom fast tears then gushed and fell:
Many will relent no more,
Who sobbed like infants then: aye, all
Who thronged the prison's stony hall,
The rulers or the slaves of law,
Felt with a new surprise and awe
That they were human, till strong shame
Made them again become the same.
The prison blood-hounds, huge and grim,

ROSALIND AND HELEN

From human looks the infection caught,
And fondly crouched and fawned on him;
And men have heard the prisoners say,
Who in their rotting dungeons lay,
That from that hour, throughout one day,
The fierce despair and hate which kept
Their trampled bosoms almost slept:
Where, like twin vultures, they hung feeding
On each heart's wound, wide torn and bleeding, —
Because their jailors' rule, they thought,
Grew merciful, like a parent's sway.

I know not how, but we were free:
And Lionel sate alone with me,
As the carriage drove thro' the streets apace;
And we looked upon each other's face;
And the blood in our fingers intertwined
Ran like the thoughts of a single mind,
As the swift emotions went and came
Thro' the veins of each united frame.
So thro' the long long streets we passed
Of the million-peopled City vast;
Which is that desert, where each one
Seeks his mate yet is alone,
Beloved and sought and mourned of none;
Until the clear blue sky was seen,

ROSALIND AND HELEN

And the grassy meadows bright and green,
And then I sunk in his embrace,
Enclosing there a mighty space
Of love: and so we travelled on
By woods, and fields of yellow flowers,
And towns, and villages, and towers,
Day after day of happy hours.
It was the azure time of June,
When the skies are deep in the stainless noon,
And the warm and fitful breezes shake
The fresh green leaves of the hedgerow briar,
And there were odours then to make
The very breath we did respire
A liquid element, whereon
Our spirits, like delighted things
That walk the air on subtle wings,
Floated and mingled far away,
'Mid the warm winds of the sunny day.
And when the evening star came forth
Above the curve of the new bent moon,
And light and sound ebbed from the earth,
Like the tide of the full and weary sea
To the depths of its tranquillity,
Our natures to its own repose
Did the earth's breathless sleep attune:
Like flowers, which on each other close

ROSALIND AND HELEN

Their languid leaves when daylight's gone,
We lay, till new emotions came,
Which seemed to make each mortal frame
One soul of interwoven flame,
A life in life, a second birth
In worlds diviner far than earth,
Which, like two strains of harmony
That mingle in the silent sky
Then slowly disunite, passed by
And left the tenderness of tears,
A soft oblivion of all fears,
A sweet sleep: so we travelled on
Till we came to the home of Lionel,
Among the mountains wild and lone,
Beside the hoary western sea,
Which near the verge of the echoing shore
The massy forest shadowed o'er.

The ancient steward, with hair all hoar,
As we alighted, wept to see
His master changed so fearfully;
And the old man's sobs did waken me
From my dream of unremaining gladness;
The truth flashed o'er me like quick madness
When I looked, and saw that there was death
On Lionel: yet day by day

ROSALIND AND HELEN

He lived, till fear grew hope and faith,
And in my soul I dared to say,
Nothing so bright can pass away:
Death is dark, and foul, and dull,
But he is—O how beautiful!
Yet day by day he grew more weak,
And his sweet voice, when he might speak,
Which ne'er was loud, became more low;
And the light which flashed through his waxen cheek
Grew faint, as the rose-like hues which flow
From sunset o'er the Alpine snow:
And death seemed not like death in him,
For the spirit of life o'er every limb
Lingered, a mist of sense and thought.
When the summer wind faint odours brought
From mountain flowers, even as it passed
His cheek would change, as the noonday sea
Which the dying breeze sweeps fitfully.
If but a cloud the sky o'ercast,
You might see his colour come and go,
And the softest strain of music made
Sweet smiles, yet sad, arise and fade
Amid the dew of his tender eyes;
And the breath, with intermitting flow,
Made his pale lips quiver and part.
You might hear the beatings of his heart,

ROSALIND AND HELEN

Quick, but not strong; and with my tresses
When oft he playfully would bind
In the bowers of mossy lonelinesses
His neck, and win me so to mingle
In the sweet depth of woven caresses,
And our faint limbs were intertwined,
Alas! the unquiet life did tingle
From mine own heart through every vein,
Like a captive in dreams of liberty,
Who beats the walls of his stony cell.
But his, it seemed already free,
Like the shadow of fire surrounding me!
On my faint eyes and limbs did dwell
That spirit as it passed, till soon,
As a frail cloud wandering o'er the moon,
Beneath its light invisible,
Is seen when it folds its gray wings again
To alight on midnight's dusky plain,
I lived and saw, and the gathering soul
Passed from beneath that strong control,
And I fell on a life which was sick with fear
Of all the woe that now I bear.

Amid a bloomless myrtle wood,
On a green and sea-girt promontory,
Not far from where we dwelt, there stood

ROSALIND AND HELEN

In record of a sweet sad story,
An altar and a temple bright
Circled by steps, and o'er the gate
Was sculptured, 'To Fidelity;'
And in the shrine an image sate,
All veiled: but there was seen the light
Of smiles, which faintly could express
A mingled pain and tenderness
Through that ethereal drapery.
The left hand held the head, the right—
Beyond the veil, beneath the skin,
You might see the nerves quivering within—
Was forcing the point of a barbèd dart
Into its side-convulsing heart.
An unskilled hand, yet one informed
With genius, had the marble warmed
With that pathetic life. This tale
It told: A dog had from the sea,
When the tide was raging fearfully,
Dragged Lionel's mother, weak and pale,
Then died beside her on the sand,
And she that temple thence had planned;
But it was Lionel's own hand
Had wrought the image. Each new moon
That lady did, in this lone fane,
The rites of a religion sweet,

ROSALIND AND HELEN

Whose god was in her heart and brain:
The seasons' loveliest flowers were strewn
On the marble floor beneath her feet,
And she brought crowns of sea-buds white,
Whose odour is so sweet and faint,
And weeds, like branching chrysolite,
Woven in devices fine and quaint,
And tears from her brown eyes did stain
The altar: need but look upon
That dying statue fair and wan,
If tears should cease, to weep again:
And rare Arabian odours came,
Through the myrtle copses steaming thence
From the hissing frankincense,
Whose smoke, wool-white as ocean foam,
Hung in dense flocks beneath the dome—
That ivory dome, whose azure night
With golden stars, like heaven, was bright—
O'er the split cedar's pointed flame;
And the lady's harp would kindle there
The melody of an old air,
Softer than sleep; the villagers
Mixed their religion up with hers,
And as they listened round, shed tears.

One eve he led me to this fane:

ROSALIND AND HELEN

Daylight on its last purple cloud
Was lingering gray, and soon her strain
The nightingale began; now loud,
Climbing in circles the windless sky,
Now dying music; suddenly
'Tis scattered in a thousand notes,
And now to the hushed ear it floats
Like field smells known in infancy,
Then failing, soothes the air again.
We sate within that temple lone,
Pavilioned round with Parian stone:
His mother's harp stood near, and oft
I had awakened music soft
Amid its wires: the nightingale
Was pausing in her heaven-taught tale:
'Now drain the cup,' said Lionel,
'Which the poet-bird has crowned so well
With the wine of her bright and liquid song!
Heardst thou not sweet words among
That heaven-resounding minstrelsy?
Heardst thou not, that those who die
Awake in a world of ecstasy?
That love, when limbs are interwoven,
And sleep, when the night of life is cloven,
And thought, to the world's dim boundaries clinging,
And music, when one beloved is singing,

ROSALIND AND HELEN

Is death? Let us drain right joyously
The cup which the sweet bird fills for me.'
He paused, and to my lips he bent
His own: like spirit his words went
Through all my limbs with the speed of fire;
And his keen eyes, glittering through mine,
Filled me with the flame divine,
Which in their orbs was burning far,
Like the light of an unmeasured star,
In the sky of midnight dark and deep:
Yes, 'twas his soul that did inspire
Sounds, which my skill could ne'er awaken;
And first, I felt my fingers sweep
The harp, and a long quivering cry
Burst from my lips in symphony:
The dusk and solid air was shaken,
As swift and swifter the notes came
From my touch, that wandered like quick flame,
And from my bosom, labouring
With some unutterable thing:
The awful sound of my own voice made
My faint lips tremble; in some mood
Of wordless thought Lionel stood
So pale, that even beside his cheek
The snowy column from its shade
Caught whiteness: yet his countenance

ROSALIND AND HELEN

Raised upward, burned with radiance
Of spirit-piercing joy, whose light,
Like the moon struggling through the night
Of whirlwind-rifted clouds, did break
With beams that might not be confined.
I paused, but soon his gestures kindled
New power, as by the moving wind
The waves are lifted, and my song
To low soft notes now changed and dwindled,
And from the twinkling wires among,
My languid fingers drew and flung
Circles of life-dissolving sound,
Yet faint; in aëry rings they bound
My Lionel, who, as every strain
Grew fainter but more sweet, his mien
Sunk with the sound relaxedly;
And slowly now he turned to me,
As slowly faded from his face
That awful joy: with looks serene
He was soon drawn to my embrace,
And my wild song then died away
In murmurs: words I dare not say
We mixed, and on his lips mine fed
Till they methought felt still and cold:
'What is it with thee, love?' I said:
No word, no look, no motion! yes,

64

ROSALIND AND HELEN

There was a change, but spare to guess,
Nor let that moment's hope be told.
I looked, and knew that he was dead,
And fell, as the eagle on the plain
Falls when life deserts her brain,
And the mortal lightning is veiled again.

O that I were now dead! but such
(Did they not, love, demand too much,
Those dying murmurs?) he forbade.
O that I once again were mad!
And yet, dear Rosalind, not so,
For I would live to share thy woe.
Sweet boy, did I forget thee too?
Alas, we know not what we do
When we speak words.
                No memory more
Is in my mind of that sea shore.
Madness came on me, and a troop
Of misty shapes did seem to sit
Beside me, on a vessel's poop,
And the clear north wind was driving it.
Then I heard strange tongues, and saw strange flowers,
And the stars methought grew unlike ours,
And the azure sky and the stormless sea
Made me believe that I had died,

f.II

ROSALIND AND HELEN

And waked in a world, which was to me
Drear hell, though heaven to all beside:
Then a dead sleep fell on my mind,
Whilst animal life many long years
Had rescue from a chasm of tears;
And when I woke, I wept to find
That the same lady, bright and wise,
With silver locks and quick brown eyes,
The mother of my Lionel,
Had tended me in my distress,
And died some months before. Nor less
Wonder, but far more peace and joy
Brought in that hour my lovely boy;
For through that trance my soul had well
The impress of thy being kept;
And if I waked, or if I slept,
No doubt, though memory faithless be,
Thy image ever dwelt on me;
And thus, O Lionel, like thee
Is our sweet child. 'Tis sure most strange
I knew not of so great a change,
As that which gave him birth, who now
Is all the solace of my woe.

That Lionel great wealth had left
By will to me, and that of all

ROSALIND AND HELEN

The ready lies of law bereft
My child and me, might well befall.
But let me think not of the scorn,
Which from the meanest I have borne,
When, for my child's belovèd sake,
I mixed with slaves, to vindicate
The very laws themselves do make:
Let me not say scorn is my fate,
Lest I be proud, suffering the same
With those who live in deathless fame.

She ceased. — 'Lo, where red morning thro' the woods
Is burning o'er the dew;' said Rosalind.
And with these words they rose, and towards the flood
Of the blue lake, beneath the leaves now wind
With equal steps and fingers intertwined:
Thence to a lonely dwelling, where the shore
Is shadowed with deep rocks, and cypresses
Cleave with their dark green cones the silent skies,
And with their shadows the clear depths below,
And where a little terrace from its bowers,
Of blooming myrtle and faint lemon-flowers,
Scatters its sense-dissolving fragrance o'er
The liquid marble of the windless lake;
And where the agèd forest's limbs look hoar,
Under the leaves which their green garments make,

ROSALIND AND HELEN

They come: 'tis Helen's home, and clean and white,
Like one which tyrants spare on our own land
In some such solitude, its casements bright
Shone through their vine-leaves in the morning sun,
And even within 'twas scarce like Italy.
And when she saw how all things there were planned,
As in an English home, dim memory
Disturbed poor Rosalind: she stood as one
Whose mind is where his body cannot be,
Till Helen led her where her child yet slept,
And said, 'Observe, that brow was Lionel's,
Those lips were his, and so he ever kept
One arm in sleep, pillowing his head with it.
You cannot see his eyes, they are two wells
Of liquid love: let us not wake him yet.'
But Rosalind could bear no more, and wept
A shower of burning tears, which fell upon
His face, and so his opening lashes shone
With tears unlike his own, as he did leap
In sudden wonder from his innocent sleep.

So Rosalind and Helen lived together
Thenceforth, changed in all else, yet friends again,
Such as they were, when o'er the mountain heather
They wandered in their youth, through sun and rain.
And after many years, for human things

ROSALIND AND HELEN

Change even like the ocean and the wind,
Her daughter was restored to Rosalind,
And in their circle thence some visitings
Of joy 'mid their new calm would intervene:
A lovely child she was, of looks serene,
And motions which o'er things indifferent shed
The grace and gentleness from whence they came.
And Helen's boy grew with her, and they fed
From the same flowers of thought, until each mind
Like springs which mingle in one flood became,
And in their union soon their parents saw
The shadow of the peace denied to them.
And Rosalind, for when the living stem
Is cankered in its heart, the tree must fall,
Died ere her time; and with deep grief and awe
The pale survivors followed her remains
Beyond the region of dissolving rains,
Up the cold mountain she was wont to call
Her tomb; and on Chiavenna's precipice
They raised a pyramid of lasting ice,
Whose polished sides, ere day had yet begun,
Caught the first glow of the unrisen sun,
The last, when it had sunk; and thro' the night
The charioteers of Arctos wheelèd round
Its glittering point, as seen from Helen's home,
Whose sad inhabitants each year would come,

ROSALIND AND HELEN

With willing steps climbing that rugged height,
And hang long locks of hair, and garlands bound
With amaranth flowers, which, in the clime's despite,
Filled the frore air with unaccustomed light:
Such flowers, as in the wintry memory bloom
Of one friend left, adorned that frozen tomb.

Helen, whose spirit was of softer mould,
Whose sufferings too were less, Death slowlier led
Into the peace of his dominion cold:
She died among her kindred, being old.
And know, that if love die not in the dead
As in the living, none of mortal kind
Are blest, as now Helen and Rosalind.

1817-1818.

THE WOODMAN AND THE NIGHTINGALE

A WOODMAN whose rough heart was out of tune
(I think such hearts yet never came to good)
Hated to hear, under the stars or moon,

One nightingale in an interfluous wood
Satiate the hungry dark with melody;—
And as a vale is watered by a flood,

Or as the moonlight fills the open sky
Struggling with darkness—as a tuberose
Peoples some Indian dell with scents which lie

Like clouds above the flower from which they rose,
The singing of that happy nightingale
In this sweet forest, from the golden close

Of evening till the star of dawn may fail,
Was interfused upon the silentness;
The folded roses and the violets pale

Heard her within their slumbers, the abyss
Of heaven with all its planets; the dull ear
Of the night-cradled earth; the loneliness

Of the circumfluous waters,—every sphere
And every flower and beam and cloud and wave,
And every wind of the mute atmosphere,

THE WOODMAN AND THE NIGHTINGALE

And every beast stretched in its ruggèd cave,
And every bird lulled on its mossy bough,
And every silver moth fresh from the grave

Which is its cradle—ever from below
Aspiring like one who loves too fair, too far,
To be consumed within the purest glow

Of one serene and unapproachèd star,
As if it were a lamp of earthly light,
Unconscious, as some human lovers are,

Itself how low, how high beyond all height
The heaven where it would perish!—and every form
That worshipped in the temple of the night

Was awed into delight, and by the charm
Girt as with an interminable zone,
Whilst that sweet bird, whose music was a storm

Of sound, shook forth the dull oblivion
Out of their dreams; harmony became love
In every soul but one.

.   .   .   .

And so this man returned with axe and saw
At evening close from killing the tall treen,
The soul of whom by Nature's gentle law

THE WOODMAN AND THE NIGHTINGALE

Was each a wood-nymph, and kept ever green
The pavement and the roof of the wild copse,
Chequering the sunlight of the blue serene

With jaggèd leaves, —and from the forest tops
Singing the winds to sleep—or weeping oft
Fast showers of aëreal water-drops

Into their mother's bosom, sweet and soft,
Nature's pure tears which have no bitterness;—
Around the cradles of the birds aloft

They spread themselves into the loveliness
Of fan-like leaves, and over pallid flowers
Hang like moist clouds:—or, where high branches kiss,

Make a green space among the silent bowers,
Like a vast fane in a metropolis,
Surrounded by the columns and the towers

All overwrought with branch-like traceries
In which there is religion—and the mute
Persuasion of unkindled melodies,

Odours and gleams and murmurs, which the lute
Of the blind pilot-spirit of the blast
Stirs as it sails, now grave and now acute,

Wakening the leaves and waves, ere it has passed
To such brief unison as on the brain

THE WOODMAN AND THE NIGHTINGALE

One tone, which never can recur, has cast,
One accent never to return again.

.   .   .   .

The world is full of Woodmen who expel
Love's gentle Dryads from the haunts of life,
And vex the nightingales in every dell.

1818.

MARENGHI

1

LET those who pine in pride or in revenge,
  Or think that ill for ill should be repaid,
Who barter wrong for wrong, until the exchange
  Ruins the merchants of such thriftless trade,
Visit the tower of Vado, and unlearn
Such bitter faith beside Marenghi's urn.

2

A massy tower yet overhangs the town,
  A scattered group of ruined dwellings now . . . .
.   .   .   .   .

3

Another scene ere wise Etruria knew
  Its second ruin through internal strife,
And tyrants through the breach of discord threw
  The chain which binds and kills. As death to life,
As winter to fair flowers (though some be poison)
So Monarchy succeeds to Freedom's foison.

4

In Pisa's church a cup of sculptured gold
  Was brimming with the blood of feuds forsworn:
A Sacrament more holy ne'er of old

MARENGHI

Etrurians mingled mid the shades forlorn
Of moon-illumined forests, when . . . .

5

And reconciling factions wet their lips
   With that dread wine, and swear to keep each spirit
Undarkened by their country's last eclipse . . . .

    .   .   .   .   .

6

Was Florence the liberticide? that band
   Of free and glorious brothers who had planted,
Like a green isle mid Aethiopian sand,
   A nation amid slaveries, disenchanted
Of many impious faiths—wise, just—do they,
Does Florence, gorge the sated tyrants' prey?

7

O foster-nurse of man's abandoned glory,
   Since Athens, its great mother, sunk in splendour;
Thou shadowest forth that mighty shape in story,
   As ocean its wrecked fanes, severe yet tender:—
The light-invested angel Poesy
Was drawn from the dim world to welcome thee.

8

And thou in painting did transcribe all taught
   By loftiest meditations; marble knew

76

MARENGHI

The sculptor's fearless soul—and as he wrought,
   The grace of his own power and freedom grew.
And more than all, heroic, just, sublime,
Thou wert among the false . . . was this thy crime?

9

Yes; and on Pisa's marble walls the twine
   Of direst weeds hangs garlanded—the snake
Inhabits its wrecked palaces;—in thine
   A beast of subtler venom now doth make
Its lair, and sits amid their glories overthrown,
And thus thy victim's fate is as thine own.

10

The sweetest flowers are ever frail and rare,
   And love and freedom blossom but to wither;
And good and ill like vines entangled are,
   So that their grapes may oft be plucked together;—
Divide the vintage ere thou drink, then make
Thy heart rejoice for dead Marenghi's sake.

10a

[Albert] Marenghi was a Florentine;
   If he had wealth, or children, or a wife
Or friends, [or farm] or cherished thoughts which twine
   The sights and sounds of home with life's own life
Of these he was despoiled and Florence sent . . . .

    .   .   .   .   .

MARENGHI

11

No record of his crime remains in story,
   But if the morning bright as evening shone,
It was some high and holy deed, by glory
   Pursued into forgetfulness, which won
From the blind crowd he made secure and free
The patriot's meed, toil, death, and infamy.

12

For when by sound of trumpet was declared
   A price upon his life, and there was set
A penalty of blood on all who shared
   So much of water with him as might wet
His lips, which speech divided not—he went
Alone, as you may guess, to banishment.

13

Amid the mountains, like a hunted beast,
   He hid himself, and hunger, toil, and cold,
Month after month endured; it was a feast
   Whene'er he found those globes of deep-red gold
Which in the woods the strawberry-tree doth bear,
Suspended in their emerald atmosphere.

14

And in the roofless huts of vast morasses,
   Deserted by the fever-stricken serf,

MARENGHI

All overgrown with reeds and long rank grasses,
　　And hillocks heaped of moss-inwoven turf,
And where the huge and speckled aloe made,
Rooted in stones, a broad and pointed shade, —

15

He housed himself. There is a point of strand
　　Near Vado's tower and town; and on one side
The treacherous marsh divides it from the land,
　　Shadowed by pine and ilex forests wide,
And on the other, creeps eternally,
Through muddy weeds, the shallow sullen sea.

16

Here the earth's breath is pestilence, and few
　　But things whose nature is at war with life—
Snakes and ill worms—endure its mortal dew.
　　The trophies of the clime's victorious strife—
And ringed horns which the buffalo did wear,
And the wolf's dark gray scalp who tracked him there.

17

And at the utmost point . . . stood there
　　The relics of a reed-inwoven cot,
Thatched with broad flags. An outlawed murderer
　　Had lived seven days there: the pursuit was hot

MARENGHI

When he was cold. The birds that were his grave
Fell dead after their feast in Vado's wave.

18

There must have burned within Marenghi's breast
   That fire, more warm and bright than life and hope,
(Which to the martyr makes his dungeon . . . .
   More joyous than free heaven's majestic cope
To his oppressor), warring with decay, —
Or he could ne'er have lived years, day by day.

19

Nor was his state so lone as you might think.
   He had tamed every newt and snake and toad,
And every seagull which sailed down to drink
   Those freshes ere the death-mist went abroad.
And each one, with peculiar talk and play,
Wiled, not untaught, his silent time away.

20

And the marsh-meteors, like tame beasts, at night
   Came licking with blue tongues his veinèd feet:
And he would watch them, as, like spirits bright,
   In many entangled figures quaint and sweet
To some enchanted music they would dance—
Until they vanished at the first moon-glance.

MARENGHI

21

He mocked the stars by grouping on each weed
  The summer dew-globes in the golden dawn;
And, ere the hoar-frost languished, he could read
  Its pictured path, as on bare spots of lawn
Its delicate brief touch in silver weaves
The likeness of the wood's remembered leaves.

22

And many a fresh Spring morn would he awaken—
  While yet the unrisen sun made glow, like iron
Quivering in crimson fire, the peaks unshaken
  Of mountains and blue isles which did environ
With air-clad crags that plain of land and sea, —
And feel   liberty.

23

And in the moonless nights, when the dun ocean
  Heaved underneath wide heaven, star-impearled,
Starting from dreams . . .
  Communed with the immeasurable world;
And felt his life beyond his limbs dilated,
Till his mind grew like that it contemplated.

24

His food was the wild fig and strawberry;
  The milky pine-nuts which the autumn-blast

MARENGHI

Shakes into the tall grass; or such small fry
    As from the sea by winter-storms are cast;
And the coarse bulbs of iris-flowers he found
Knotted in clumps under the spongy ground.

25

And so were kindled powers and thoughts which made
    His solitude less dark. When memory came
(For years gone by leave each a deepening shade),
    His spirit basked in its internal flame, —
As, when the black storm hurries round at night,
The fisher basks beside his red firelight.

26

Yet human hopes and cares and faiths and errors,
    Like billows unawakened by the wind,
Slept in Marenghi still; but that all terrors,
    Weakness, and doubt, had withered in his mind.
His couch . . .

    .   .   .   .   .

27

And, when he saw beneath the sunset's planet
    A black ship walk over the crimson ocean, —
Its pennon streaming on the blasts that fan it,
    Its sails and ropes all tense and without motion,

MARENGHI

Like the dark ghost of the unburied even
Striding athwart the orange-coloured heaven, —

28

The thought of his own kind who made the soul
   Which sped that wingèd shape through night and day, —
The thought of his own country . . .

      .   .   .   .   .

                                   1818.

JULIAN AND MADDALO

A CONVERSATION

*

PREFACE

The meadows with fresh streams, the bees with thyme,
The goats with the green leaves of budding Spring,
Are saturated not — nor Love with tears.

Virgil's ' Gallus.'

COUNT MADDALO is a Venetian nobleman of
ancient family and of great fortune, who, without
mixing much in the society of his countrymen, resides
chiefly at his magnificent palace in that city. He is a
person of the most consummate genius, and capable, if
he would direct his energies to such an end, of becoming
the redeemer of his degraded country. But it is his weak-
ness to be proud : he derives, from a comparison of his
own extraordinary mind with the dwarfish intellects that
surround him, an intense apprehension of the nothing-
ness of human life. His passions and his powers are
incomparably greater than those of other men; and,
instead of the latter having been employed in curbing
the former, they have mutually lent each other strength.
His ambition preys upon itself, for want of objects which
it can consider worthy of exertion. I say that Maddalo

84

is proud, because I can find no other word to express
the concentered and impatient feelings which consume
him; but it is on his own hopes and affections only that
he seems to trample, for in social life no human being
can be more gentle, patient, and unassuming than
Maddalo. He is cheerful, frank, and witty. His more
serious conversation is a sort of intoxication; men are
held by it as by a spell. He has travelled much; and
there is an inexpressible charm in his relation of his ad-
ventures in different countries.

Julian is an Englishman of good family, passionately
attached to those philosophical notions which assert the
power of man over his own mind, and the immense im-
provements of which, by the extinction of certain moral
superstitions, human society may be yet susceptible.
Without concealing the evil in the world, he is for ever
speculating how good may be made superior. He is a
complete infidel, and a scoffer at all things reputed holy;
and Maddalo takes a wicked pleasure in drawing out
his taunts against religion. What Maddalo thinks on
these matters is not exactly known. Julian, in spite of his
heterodox opinions, is conjectured by his friends to
possess some good qualities. How far this is possible the
pious reader will determine. Julian is rather serious.

Of the Maniac I can give no information. He seems,
by his own account, to have been disappointed in love.

JULIAN AND MADDALO

He was evidently a very cultivated and amiable person when in his right senses. His story, told at length, might be like many other stories of the same kind: the unconnected exclamations of his agony will perhaps be found a sufficient comment for the text of every heart.

I RODE one evening with Count Maddalo
Upon the bank of land which breaks the flow
Of Adria towards Venice: a bare strand
Of hillocks, heaped from ever-shifting sand,
Matted with thistles and amphibious weeds,
Such as from earth's embrace the salt ooze breeds,
Is this; an uninhabited sea-side,
Which the lone fisher, when his nets are dried,
Abandons; and no other object breaks
The waste, but one dwarf tree and some few stakes
Broken and unrepaired, and the tide makes
A narrow space of level sand thereon,
Where 'twas our wont to ride while day went down.
This ride was my delight. I love all waste
And solitary places ; where we taste
The pleasure of believing what we see
Is boundless, as we wish our souls to be:
And such was this wide ocean, and this shore
More barren than its billows; and yet more
Than all, with a remembered friend I love
To ride as then I rode ;—for the winds drove
The living spray along the sunny air
Into our faces; the blue heavens were bare,
Stripped to their depths by the awakening north;
And, from the waves, sound like delight broke forth

JULIAN AND MADDALO

Harmonising with solitude, and sent
Into our hearts aëreal merriment.
So, as we rode, we talked; and the swift thought,
Winging itself with laughter, lingered not,
But flew from brain to brain,—such glee was ours,
Charged with light memories of remembered hours,
None slow enough for sadness: till we came
Homeward, which always makes the spirit tame.
This day had been cheerful but cold, and now
The sun was sinking, and the wind also.
Our talk grew somewhat serious, as may be
Talk interrupted with such raillery
As mocks itself, because it cannot scorn
The thoughts it would extinguish:—'twas forlorn,
Yet pleasing, such as once, so poets tell,
The devils held within the dales of Hell
Concerning God, freewill and destiny:
Of all that earth has been or yet may be,
All that vain men imagine or believe,
Or hope can paint or suffering may achieve,
We descanted, and I (for ever still
Is it not wise to make the best of ill?)
Argued against despondency, but pride
Made my companion take the darker side.
The sense that he was greater than his kind
Had struck, methinks, his eagle spirit blind

88

JULIAN AND MADDALO

By gazing on its own exceeding light.
Meanwhile the sun paused ere it should alight,
Over the horizon of the mountains;—Oh,
How beautiful is sunset, when the glow
Of Heaven descends upon a land like thee,
Thou Paradise of exiles, Italy!
Thy mountains, seas, and vineyards, and the towers
Of cities they encircle!—it was ours
To stand on thee, beholding it: and then,
Just where we had dismounted, the Count's men
Were waiting for us with the gondola.—
As those who pause on some delightful way
Though bent on pleasant pilgrimage, we stood
Looking upon the evening, and the flood
Which lay between the city and the shore,
Paved with the image of the sky . . . the hoar
And aëry Alps towards the North appeared
Through mist, an heaven-sustaining bulwark reared
Between the East and West; and half the sky
Was roofed with clouds of rich emblazonry
Dark purple at the zenith, which still grew
Down the steep West into a wondrous hue
Brighter than burning gold, even to the rent
Where the swift sun yet paused in his descent
Among the many-folded hills: they were
Those famous Euganean hills, which bear,

JULIAN AND MADDALO

As seen from Lido thro' the harbour piles,
The likeness of a clump of peakèd isles—
And then—as if the Earth and Sea had been
Dissolved into one lake of fire, were seen
Those mountains towering as from waves of flame
Around the vaporous sun, from which there came
The inmost purple spirit of light, and made
Their very peaks transparent. 'Ere it fade,'
Said my companion, 'I will show you soon
A better station'—so, o'er the lagune
We glided; and from that funereal bark
I leaned, and saw the city, and could mark
How from their many isles, in evening's gleam,
Its temples and its palaces did seem
Like fabrics of enchantment piled to Heaven.
I was about to speak, when—'We are even
Now at the point I meant,' said Maddalo,
And bade the gondolieri cease to row.
'Look, Julian, on the west, and listen well
If you hear not a deep and heavy bell.'
I looked, and saw between us and the sun
A building on an island; such a one
As age to age might add, for uses vile,
A windowless, deformed and dreary pile;
And on the top an open tower, where hung
A bell, which in the radiance swayed and swung;

90

JULIAN AND MADDALO

We could just hear its hoarse and iron tongue:
The broad sun sunk behind it, and it tolled
In strong and black relief. —'What we behold
Shall be the madhouse and its belfry tower,'
Said Maddalo, 'and ever at this hour
Those who may cross the water, hear that bell
Which calls the maniacs, each one from his cell,
To vespers.'—'As much skill as need to pray
In thanks or hope for their dark lot have they
To their stern maker,' I replied. 'O ho!
You talk as in years past,' said Maddalo.
''Tis strange men change not. You were ever still
Among Christ's flock a perilous infidel,
A wolf for the meek lambs—if you can't swim
Beware of Providence.' I looked on him,
But the gay smile had faded in his eye.
'And such,'—he cried, 'is our mortality,
And this must be the emblem and the sign
Of what should be eternal and divine!—
And like that black and dreary bell, the soul,
Hung in a heaven-illumined tower, must toll
Our thoughts and our desires to meet below
Round the rent heart and pray—as madmen do
For what? they know not,—till the night of death
As sunset that strange vision, severeth
Our memory from itself, and us from all

JULIAN AND MADDALO

We sought and yet were baffled.' I recall
The sense of what he said, although I mar
The force of his expressions. The broad star
Of day meanwhile had sunk behind the hill,
And the black bell became invisible,
And the red tower looked gray, and all between
The churches, ships and palaces were seen
Huddled in gloom;—into the purple sea
The orange hues of heaven sunk silently.
We hardly spoke, and soon the gondola
Conveyed me to my lodging by the way.
    The following morn was rainy, cold and dim:
Ere Maddalo arose, I called on him,
And whilst I waited with his child I played;
A lovelier toy sweet Nature never made,
A serious, subtle, wild, yet gentle being,
Graceful without design and unforeseeing,
With eyes—Oh speak not of her eyes!—which seem
Twin mirrors of Italian Heaven, yet gleam
With such deep meaning, as we never see
But in the human countenance: with me
She was a special favourite: I had nursed
Her fine and feeble limbs when she came first
To this bleak world; and she yet seemed to know
On second sight her ancient playfellow,
Less changed than she was by six months or so;

JULIAN AND MADDALO

For after her first shyness was worn out
We sate there, rolling billiard balls about,
When the Count entered. Salutations past—
'The word you spoke last night might well have cast
A darkness on my spirit—if man be
The passive thing you say, I should not see
Much harm in the religions and old saws
(Tho' I may never own such leaden laws)
Which break a teachless nature to the yoke:
Mine is another faith'—thus much I spoke
And noting he replied not, added: 'See
This lovely child, blithe, innocent and free;
She spends a happy time with little care,
While we to such sick thoughts subjected are
As came on you last night—it is our will
That thus enchains us to permitted ill—
We might be otherwise—we might be all
We dream of happy, high, majestical.
Where is the love, beauty, and truth we seek
But in our mind? and if we were not weak
Should we be less in deed than in desire?'
'Ay, if we were not weak—and we aspire
How vainly to be strong!' said Maddalo:
'You talk Utopia.' 'It remains to know,'
I then rejoined, 'and those who try may find
How strong the chains are which our spirit bind;

JULIAN AND MADDALO

Brittle perchance as straw . . . We are assured
Much may be conquered, much may be endured,
Of what degrades and crushes us. We know
That we have power over ourselves to do
And suffer—what, we know not till we try;
But something nobler than to live and die—
So taught those kings of old philosophy
Who reigned, before Religion made men blind;
And those who suffer with their suffering kind
Yet feel their faith, religion.' 'My dear friend,'
Said Maddalo, 'my judgement will not bend
To your opinion, though I think you might
Make such a system refutation-tight
As far as words go. I knew one like you
Who to this city came some months ago,
With whom I argued in this sort, and he
Is now gone mad,—and so he answered me,—
Poor fellow! but if you would like to go
We'll visit him, and his wild talk will show
How vain are such aspiring theories.'
'I hope to prove the induction otherwise,
And that a want of that true theory, still,
Which seeks a "soul of goodness" in things ill
Or in himself or others, has thus bowed
His being—there are some by nature proud,
Who patient in all else demand but this—

JULIAN AND MADDALO

To love and be beloved with gentleness;
And being scorned, what wonder if they die
Some living death? this is not destiny
But man's own wilful ill.'
                              As thus I spoke
Servants announced the gondola, and we
Through the fast-falling rain and high-wrought sea
Sailed to the island where the madhouse stands.
We disembarked. The clap of tortured hands,
Fierce yells and howlings and lamentings keen,
And laughter where complaint had merrier been,
Moans, shrieks, and curses, and blaspheming prayers
Accosted us. We climbed the oozy stairs
Into an old courtyard. I heard on high,
Then, fragments of most touching melody,
But looking up saw not the singer there—
Through the black bars in the tempestuous air
I saw, like weeds on a wrecked palace growing,
Long tangled locks flung wildly forth, and flowing,
Of those who on a sudden were beguiled
Into strange silence, and looked forth and smiled
Hearing sweet sounds. —Then I: 'Methinks there were
A cure of these with patience and kind care,
If music can thus move . . . but what is he
Whom we seek here?' 'Of his sad history
I know but this,' said Maddalo: 'he came

JULIAN AND MADDALO

To Venice a dejected man, and fame
Said he was wealthy, or he had been so;
Some thought the loss of fortune wrought him woe;
But he was ever talking in such sort
As you do—far more sadly—he seemed hurt,
Even as a man with his peculiar wrong,
To hear but of the oppression of the strong,
Or those absurd deceits (I think with you
In some respects, you know) which carry through
The excellent impostors of this earth
When they outface detection—he had worth,
Poor fellow! but a humourist in his way'—
'Alas, what drove him mad?' 'I cannot say:
A lady came with him from France, and when
She left him and returned, he wandered then
About yon lonely isles of desert sand
Till he grew wild—he had no cash or land
Remaining,—the police had brought him here—
Some fancy took him and he would not bear
Removal; so I fitted up for him
Those rooms beside the sea, to please his whim,
And sent him busts and books and urns for flowers,
Which had adorned his life in happier hours,
And instruments of music—you may guess
A stranger could do little more or less
For one so gentle and unfortunate:

96

JULIAN AND MADDALO

And those are his sweet strains which charm the weight
From madmen's chains, and make this Hell appear
A heaven of sacred silence, hushed to hear.'—
'Nay, this was kind of you—he had no claim,
As the world says'—'None—but the very same
Which I on all mankind were I as he
Fallen to such deep reverse;—his melody
Is interrupted—now we hear the din
Of madmen, shriek on shriek, again begin;
Let us now visit him; after this strain
He ever communes with himself again,
And sees nor hears not any.' Having said
These words we called the keeper, and he led
To an apartment opening on the sea—
There the poor wretch was sitting mournfully
Near a piano, his pale fingers twined
One with the other, and the ooze and wind
Rushed through an open casement, and did sway
His hair, and starred it with the brackish spray;
His head was leaning on a music book,
And he was muttering, and his lean limbs shook;
His lips were pressed against a folded leaf
In hue too beautiful for health, and grief
Smiled in their motions as they lay apart—
As one who wrought from his own fervid heart
The eloquence of passion, soon he raised

JULIAN AND MADDALO

His sad meek face and eyes lustrous and glazed
And spoke—sometimes as one who wrote, and thought
His words might move some heart that heeded not,
If sent to distant lands: and then as one
Reproaching deeds never to be undone
With wondering self-compassion; then his speech
Was lost in grief, and then his words came each
Unmodulated, cold, expressionless, —
But that from one jarred accent you might guess
It was despair made them so uniform:
And all the while the loud and gusty storm
Hissed through the window, and we stood behind
Stealing his accents from the envious wind
Unseen. I yet remember what he said
Distinctly: such impression his words made.

'Month after month,' he cried, 'to bear this load
And as a jade urged by the whip and goad
To drag life on, which like a heavy chain
Lengthens behind with many a link of pain!—
And not to speak my grief—O, not to dare
To give a human voice to my despair,
But live and move, and, wretched thing! smile on
As if I never went aside to groan,
And wear this mask of falsehood even to those
Who are most dear—not for my own repose—

JULIAN AND MADDALO

Alas! no scorn or pain or hate could be
So heavy as that falsehood is to me —
But that I cannot bear more altered faces
Than needs must be, more changed and cold embraces,
More misery, disappointment, and mistrust
To own me for their father . . . Would the dust
Were covered in upon my body now!
That the life ceased to toil within my brow!
And then these thoughts would at the least be fled;
Let us not fear such pain can vex the dead.

   ‘ What Power delights to torture us ? I know
That to myself I do not wholly owe
What now I suffer, though in part I may.
Alas! none strewed sweet flowers upon the way
Where wandering heedlessly, I met pale Pain
My shadow, which will leave me not again—
If I have erred, there was no joy in error,
But pain and insult and unrest and terror;
I have not as some do, bought penitence
With pleasure, and a dark yet sweet offence,
For then, — if love and tenderness and truth
Had overlived hope's momentary youth,
My creed should have redeemed me from repenting;
But loathèd scorn and outrage unrelenting
Met love excited by far other seeming

JULIAN AND MADDALO

Until the end was gained . . . as one from dreaming
Of sweetest peace, I woke, and found my state
Such as it is. —
               'O Thou, my spirit's mate
Who, for thou art compassionate and wise,
Wouldst pity me from thy most gentle eyes
If this sad writing thou shouldst ever see—
My secret groans must be unheard by thee,
Thou wouldst weep tears bitter as blood to know
Thy lost friend's incommunicable woe.

    'Ye few by whom my nature has been weighed
In friendship, let me not that name degrade
By placing on your hearts the secret load
Which crushes mine to dust. There is one road
To peace and that is truth, which follow ye!
Love sometimes leads astray to misery.
Yet think not though subdued—and I may well
Say that I am subdued—that the full Hell
Within me would infect the untainted breast
Of sacred nature with its own unrest;
As some perverted beings think to find
In scorn or hate a medicine for the mind
Which scorn or hate have wounded—O how vain!
The dagger heals not but may rend again . . .
Believe that I am ever still the same

100

JULIAN AND MADDALO

In creed as in resolve, and what may tame
My heart, must leave the understanding free,
Or all would sink in this keen agony—
Nor dream that I will join the vulgar cry;
Or with my silence sanction tyranny;
Or seek a moment's shelter from my pain
In any madness which the world calls gain,
Ambition or revenge or thoughts as stern
As those which make me what I am; or turn
To avarice or misanthropy or lust . . .
Heap on me soon, O grave, thy welcome dust!
Till then the dungeon may demand its prey,
And Poverty and Shame may meet and say—
Halting beside me on the public way—
"That love-devoted youth is ours—let's sit
Beside him—he may live some six months yet."
Or the red scaffold, as our country bends,
May ask some willing victim, or ye friends
May fall under some sorrow which this heart
Or hand may share or vanquish or avert;
I am prepared—in truth with no proud joy—
To do or suffer aught, as when a boy
I did devote to justice and to love
My nature, worthless now! . . .
                              'I must remove
A veil from my pent mind. 'Tis torn aside!

JULIAN AND MADDALO

O, pallid as Death's dedicated bride,
Thou mockery which art sitting by my side,
Am I not wan like thee? at the grave's call
I haste, invited to thy wedding-ball
To greet the ghastly paramour, for whom
Thou hast deserted me . . . and made the tomb
Thy bridal bed . . . But I beside your feet
Will lie and watch ye from my winding sheet—
Thus . . . wide awake tho' dead . . . yet stay, O stay!
Go not so soon—I know not what I say—
Hear but my reasons . . I am mad, I fear,
My fancy is o'erwrought . . thou art not here . . .
Pale art thou, 'tis most true . . but thou art gone,
Thy work is finished . . . I am left alone!—

    .   .   .   .   .

'Nay, was it I who wooed thee to this breast
Which, like a serpent, thou envenomest
As in repayment of the warmth it lent?
Didst thou not seek me for thine own content?
Did not thy love awaken mine? I thought
That thou wert she who said, "You kiss me not
Ever, I fear you do not love me now"—
In truth I loved even to my overthrow
Her, who would fain forget these words: but they
Cling to her mind, and cannot pass away.

    .   .   .   .   .

JULIAN AND MADDALO

'You say that I am proud—that when I speak
My lip is tortured with the wrongs which break
The spirit it expresses . . . Never one
Humbled himself before, as I have done!
Even the instinctive worm on which we tread
Turns, though it wound not—then with prostrate head
Sinks in the dusk and writhes like me—and dies?
No: wears a living death of agonies!
As the slow shadows of the pointed grass
Mark the eternal periods, his pangs pass
Slow, ever-moving,—making moments be
As mine seem—each an immortality!

. . . . .

'That you had never seen me—never heard
My voice, and more than all had ne'er endured
The deep pollution of my loathed embrace—
That your eyes ne'er had lied love in my face—
That, like some maniac monk, I had torn out
The nerves of manhood by their bleeding root
With mine own quivering fingers, so that ne'er
Our hearts had for a moment mingled there
To disunite in horror—these were not
With thee, like some suppressed and hideous thought
Which flits athwart our musings, but can find
No rest within a pure and gentle mind . . .

JULIAN AND MADDALO

Thou sealedst them with many a bare broad word,
And searedst my memory o'er them, —for I heard
And can forget not . . . they were ministered
One after one, those curses. Mix them up
Like self-destroying poisons in one cup,
And they will make one blessing which thou ne'er
Didst imprecate for, on me, —death.

    .   .   .   .   .

                              'It were
A cruel punishment for one most cruel,
If such can love, to make that love the fuel
Of the mind's hell; hate, scorn, remorse, despair:
But *me* —whose heart a stranger's tear might wear
As water-drops the sandy fountain-stone,
Who loved and pitied all things, and could moan
For woes which others hear not, and could see
The absent with the glance of phantasy,
And with the poor and trampled sit and weep,
Following the captive to his dungeon deep;
Me —who am as a nerve o'er which do creep
The else unfelt oppressions of this earth,
And was to thee the flame upon thy hearth,
When all beside was cold—that thou on me
Shouldst rain these plagues of blistering agony—
Such curses are from lips once eloquent
With love's too partial praise—let none relent

104

JULIAN AND MADDALO

Who intend deeds too dreadful for a name
Henceforth, if an example for the same
They seek . . . for thou on me lookedst so, and so—
And didst speak thus . . and thus . . . I live to show
How much men bear and die not!

   .   .   .   .   .

          'Thou wilt tell,
With the grimace of hate, how horrible
It was to meet my love when thine grew less;
Thou wilt admire how I could e'er address
Such features to love's work . . . this taunt, though true,
(For indeed Nature nor in form nor hue
Bestowed on me her choicest workmanship)
Shall not be thy defence . . . for since thy lip
Met mine first, years long past, since thine eye kindled
With soft fire under mine, I have not dwindled
Nor changed in mind or body, or in aught
But as love changes what it loveth not
After long years and many trials.
         'How vain
Are words! I thought never to speak again,
Not even in secret,—not to my own heart—
But from my lips the unwilling accents start,
And from my pen the words flow as I write,
Dazzling my eyes with scalding tears . . . my sight
Is dim to see that charactered in vain

JULIAN AND MADDALO

On this unfeeling leaf which burns the brain
And eats into it . . . blotting all things fair
And wise and good which time had written there.

   ' Those who inflict must suffer, for they see
The work of their own hearts, and this must be
Our chastisement or recompense—O child!
I would that thine were like to be more mild
For both our wretched sakes . . . for thine the most
Who feelest already all that thou hast lost
Without the power to wish it thine again;
And as slow years pass, a funereal train
Each with the ghost of some lost hope or friend
Following it like its shadow, wilt thou bend
No thought on my dead memory?

                             ' Alas, love!
Fear me not . . . against thee I would not move
A finger in despite. Do I not live
That thou mayst have less bitter cause to grieve?
I give thee tears for scorn and love for hate;
And that thy lot may be less desolate
Than his on whom thou tramplest, I refrain
From that sweet sleep which medicines all pain.
Then, when thou speakest of me, never say
"He could forgive not." Here I cast away

JULIAN AND MADDALO

All human passions, all revenge, all pride;
I think, speak, act no ill; I do but hide
Under these words, like embers, every spark
Of that which has consumed me—quick and dark
The grave is yawning . . . as its roof shall cover
My limbs with dust and worms under and over
So let Oblivion hide this grief . . . the air
Closes upon my accents, as despair
Upon my heart—let death upon despair!'

    He ceased, and overcome leant back awhile,
Then rising, with a melancholy smile
Went to a sofa, and lay down, and slept
A heavy sleep, and in his dreams he wept
And muttered some familiar name, and we
Wept without shame in his society.
I think I never was impressed so much;
The man who were not, must have lacked a touch
Of human nature . . . then we lingered not,
Although our argument was quite forgot,
But calling the attendants, went to dine
At Maddalo's; yet neither cheer nor wine
Could give us spirits, for we talked of him
And nothing else, till daylight made stars dim;
And we agreed his was some dreadful ill
Wrought on him boldly, yet unspeakable,

JULIAN AND MADDALO

By a dear friend; some deadly change in love
Of one vowed deeply which he dreamed not of;
For whose sake he, it seemed, had fixed a blot
Of falsehood on his mind which flourished not
But in the light of all-beholding truth;
And having stamped this canker on his youth
She had abandoned him—and how much more
Might be his woe, we guessed not—he had store
Of friends and fortune once, as we could guess
From his nice habits and his gentleness;
These were now lost . . . it were a grief indeed
If he had changed one unsustaining reed
For all that such a man might else adorn.
The colours of his mind seemed yet unworn;
For the wild language of his grief was high,
Such as in measure were called poetry;
And I remember one remark which then
Maddalo made. He said: 'Most wretched men
Are cradled into poetry by wrong,
They learn in suffering what they teach in song.'

If I had been an unconnected man
I, from this moment, should have formed some plan
Never to leave sweet Venice,—for to me
It was delight to ride by the lone sea;
And then, the town is silent—one may write

108

JULIAN AND MADDALO

Or read in gondolas by day or night,
Having the little brazen lamp alight,
Unseen, uninterrupted; books are there,
Pictures, and casts from all those statues fair
Which were twin-born with poetry, and all
We seek in towns, with little to recall
Regrets for the green country. I might sit
In Maddalo's great palace, and his wit
And subtle talk would cheer the winter night
And make me know myself, and the firelight
Would flash upon our faces, till the day
Might dawn and make me wonder at my stay:
But I had friends in London too: the chief
Attraction here, was that I sought relief
From the deep tenderness that maniac wrought
Within me — 'twas perhaps an idle thought —
But I imagined that if day by day
I watched him, and but seldom went away,
And studied all the beatings of his heart
With zeal, as men study some stubborn art
For their own good, and could by patience find
An entrance to the caverns of his mind,
I might reclaim him from his dark estate:
In friendships I had been most fortunate —
Yet never saw I one whom I would call
More willingly my friend; and this was all

JULIAN AND MADDALO

Accomplished not; such dreams of baseless good
Oft come and go in crowds or solitude
And leave no trace—but what I now designed
Made for long years impression on my mind.
The following morning, urged by my affairs,
I left bright Venice.
                          After many years
And many changes I returned; the name
Of Venice, and its aspect, was the same;
But Maddalo was travelling far away
Among the mountains of Armenia.
His dog was dead. His child had now become
A woman; such as it has been my doom
To meet with few, —a wonder of this earth,
Where there is little of transcendent worth, —
Like one of Shakespeare's women: kindly she,
And, with a manner beyond courtesy,
Received her father's friend; and when I asked
Of the lorn maniac, she her memory tasked,
And told as she had heard the mournful tale:
'That the poor sufferer's health began to fail
Two years from my departure, but that then
The lady who had left him, came again.
Her mien had been imperious, but she now
Looked meek—perhaps remorse had brought her low.
Her coming made him better, and they stayed

JULIAN AND MADDALO

Together at my father's—for I played,
As I remember, with the lady's shawl—
I might be six years old—but after all
She left him'.... 'Why, her heart must have been tough:
How did it end?' 'And was not this enough?
They met—they parted'—'Child, is there no more?'
'Something within that interval which bore
The stamp of *why* they parted, *how* they met:
Yet if thine agèd eyes disdain to wet
Those wrinkled cheeks with youth's remembered tears,
Ask me no more, but let the silent years
Be closed and cered over their memory
As yon mute marble where their corpses lie.'
I urged and questioned still, she told me how
All happened—but the cold world shall not know.

1818.

THE MASK OF ANARCHY

Written on the occasion
of the massacre at
Manchester

I

AS I lay asleep in Italy
There came a voice from over the Sea,
And with great power it forth led me
To walk in the visions of Poesy.

2

I met Murder on the way—
He had a mask like Castlereagh—
Very smooth he looked, yet grim;
Seven blood-hounds followed him:

3

All were fat; and well they might
Be in admirable plight,
For one by one, and two by two,
He tossed them human hearts to chew
Which from his wide cloak he drew.

4

Next came Fraud, and he had on,
Like Eldon, an ermined gown;

THE MASK OF ANARCHY

His big tears, for he wept well,
Turned to mill-stones as they fell.

5

And the little children, who
Round his feet played to and fro,
Thinking every tear a gem,
Had their brains knocked out by them.

6

Clothed with the Bible, as with light,
And the shadows of the night,
Like Sidmouth, next, Hypocrisy
On a crocodile rode by.

7

And many more Destructions played
In this ghastly masquerade,
All disguised, even to the eyes,
Like Bishops, lawyers, peers, or spies.

8

Last came Anarchy: he rode
On a white horse, splashed with blood;
He was pale even to the lips,
Like Death in the Apocalypse.

9

And he wore a kingly crown;
And in his grasp a sceptre shone;
On his brow this mark I saw —
'I AM GOD, AND KING, AND LAW!'

10

With a pace stately and fast,
Over English land he passed,
Trampling to a mire of blood
The adoring multitude.

11

And a mighty troop around,
With their trampling shook the ground,
Waving each a bloody sword,
For the service of their Lord.

12

And with glorious triumph, they
Rode through England proud and gay,
Drunk as with intoxication
Of the wine of desolation.

13

O'er fields and towns, from sea to sea,
Passed the Pageant swift and free,

THE MASK OF ANARCHY

Tearing up, and trampling down;
Till they came to London town.

14

And each dweller, panic-stricken,
Felt his heart with terror sicken
Hearing the tempestuous cry
Of the triumph of Anarchy.

15

For with pomp to meet him came,
Clothed in arms like blood and flame,
The hired murderers, who did sing
'Thou art God, and Law, and King.

16

'We have waited, weak and lone
For thy coming, Mighty One!
Our purses are empty, our swords are cold,
Give us glory, and blood, and gold.'

17

Lawyers and priests, a motley crowd,
To the earth their pale brows bowed;
Like a bad prayer not over loud,
Whispering—'Thou art Law and God.'—

18

Then all cried with one accord,
'Thou art King, and God, and Lord;
Anarchy, to thee we bow,
Be thy name made holy now!'

19

And Anarchy, the Skeleton,
Bowed and grinned to every one,
As well as if his education
Had cost ten millions to the nation.

20

For he knew the Palaces
Of our Kings were rightly his;
His the sceptre, crown, and globe,
And the gold-inwoven robe.

21

So he sent his slaves before
To seize upon the Bank and Tower,
And was proceeding with intent
To meet his pensioned Parliament

22

When one fled past, a maniac maid,
And her name was Hope, she said:

THE MASK OF ANARCHY

But she looked more like Despair,
And she cried out in the air:

23

'My father Time is weak and gray
With waiting for a better day;
See how idiot-like he stands,
Fumbling with his palsied hands!

24

'He has had child after child,
And the dust of death is piled
Over every one but me—
Misery, oh, Misery!'

25

Then she lay down in the street,
Right before the horses' feet,
Expecting, with a patient eye,
Murder, Fraud, and Anarchy.

26

When between her and her foes
A mist, a light, an image rose,
Small at first, and weak, and frail
Like the vapour of a vale:

THE MASK OF ANARCHY

27

Till as clouds grow on the blast,
Like tower-crowned giants striding fast,
And glare with lightnings as they fly,
And speak in thunder to the sky,

28

It grew—a Shape arrayed in mail
Brighter than the viper's scale,
And upborne on wings whose grain
Was as the light of sunny rain.

29

On its helm, seen far away,
A planet, like the Morning's, lay;
And those plumes its light rained through
Like a shower of crimson dew.

30

With step as soft as wind it passed
O'er the heads of men—so fast
That they knew the presence there,
And looked,—but all was empty air.

31

As flowers beneath May's footstep waken,
As stars from Night's loose hair are shaken,

THE MASK OF ANARCHY

As waves arise when loud winds call,
Thoughts sprung where'er that step did fall.

32

And the prostrate multitude
Looked—and ankle-deep in blood,
Hope, that maiden most serene,
Was walking with a quiet mien:

33

And Anarchy, the ghastly birth,
Lay dead earth upon the earth;
The Horse of Death tameless as wind
Fled, and with his hoofs did grind
To dust the murderers thronged behind.

34

A rushing light of clouds and splendour,
A sense awakening and yet tender
Was heard and felt—and at its close
These words of joy and fear arose

35

As if their own indignant Earth
Which gave the sons of England birth
Had felt their blood upon her brow,
And shuddering with a mother's throe

36

Had turnèd every drop of blood
By which her face had been bedewed
To an accent unwithstood, —
As if her heart had cried aloud:

37

'Men of England, heirs of Glory,
Heroes of unwritten story,
Nurslings of one mighty Mother,
Hopes of her, and one another;

38

' Rise like Lions after slumber
In unvanquishable number,
Shake your chains to earth like dew
Which in sleep had fallen on you—
Ye are many—they are few.

39

'What is Freedom?—ye can tell
That which slavery is, too well—
For its very name has grown
To an echo of your own.

40

''Tis to work and have such pay
As just keeps life from day to day

THE MASK OF ANARCHY

In your limbs, as in a cell
For the tyrants' use to dwell,

41

' So that ye for them are made
Loom, and plough, and sword, and spade,
With or without your own will bent
To their defence and nourishment.

42

' 'Tis to see your children weak
With their mothers pine and peak,
When the winter winds are bleak, —
They are dying whilst I speak.

43

' 'Tis to hunger for such diet
As the rich man in his riot
Casts to the fat dogs that lie
Surfeiting beneath his eye;

44

' 'Tis to let the Ghost of Gold
Take from Toil a thousandfold
More than e'er its substance could
In the tyrannies of old.

45

'Paper coin—that forgery
Of the title-deeds, which ye
Hold to something of the worth
Of the inheritance of Earth.

46

''Tis to be a slave in soul
And to hold no strong control
Over your own wills, but be
All that others make of ye.

47

'And at length when ye complain
With a murmur weak and vain
'Tis to see the Tyrant's crew
Ride over your wives and you—
Blood is on the grass like dew.

48

'Then it is to feel revenge
Fiercely thirsting to exchange
Blood for blood—and wrong for wrong—
Do not thus when ye are strong.

49

'Birds find rest, in narrow nest
When weary of their wingèd quest;

THE MASK OF ANARCHY

Beasts find fare, in woody lair
When storm and snow are in the air.

50

'Asses, swine, have litter spread
And with fitting food are fed;
All things have a home but one—
Thou, Oh, Englishman, hast none!

51

'This is Slavery—savage men,
Or wild beasts within a den
Would endure not as ye do—
But such ills they never knew.

52

'What art thou Freedom? O! could slaves
Answer from their living graves
This demand—tyrants would flee
Like a dream's dim imagery:

53

'Thou art not, as impostors say,
A shadow soon to pass away,
A superstition, and a name
Echoing from the cave of Fame.

54

'For the labourer thou art bread,
And a comely table spread
From his daily labour come
In a neat and happy home.

55

'Thou art clothes, and fire, and food
For the trampled multitude—
No—in countries that are free
Such starvation cannot be
As in England now we see.

56

'To the rich thou art a check,
When his foot is on the neck
Of his victim, thou dost make
That he treads upon a snake.

57

'Thou art Justice—ne'er for gold
May thy righteous laws be sold
As laws are in England—thou
Shield'st alike the high and low.

58

'Thou art Wisdom—Freemen never
Dream that God will damn for ever

THE MASK OF ANARCHY

All who think those things untrue
Of which Priests make such ado.

59

'Thou art Peace—never by thee
Would blood and treasure wasted be
As tyrants wasted them, when all
Leagued to quench thy flame in Gaul.

60

'What if English toil and blood
Was poured forth, even as a flood?
It availed, Oh, Liberty,
To dim, but not extinguish thee.

61

'Thou art Love—the rich have kissed
Thy feet, and like him following Christ,
Give their substance to the free
And through the rough world follow thee,

62

'Or turn their wealth to arms, and make
War for thy belovèd sake
On wealth, and war, and fraud—whence they
Drew the power which is their prey.

63

'Science, Poetry, and Thought
Are thy lamps; they make the lot
Of the dwellers in a cot
So serene, they curse it not.

64

'Spirit, Patience, Gentleness,
All that can adorn and bless
Art thou—let deeds, not words, express
Thine exceeding loveliness.

65

'Let a great Assembly be
Of the fearless and the free
On some spot of English ground
Where the plains stretch wide around.

66

'Let the blue sky overhead,
The green earth on which ye tread,
All that must eternal be
Witness the solemnity.

67

'From the corners uttermost
Of the bounds of English coast;

THE MASK OF ANARCHY

From every hut, village, and town
Where those who live and suffer moan
For others' misery or their own,

68

' From the workhouse and the prison
Where pale as corpses newly risen,
Women, children, young and old
Groan for pain, and weep for cold—

69

' From the haunts of daily life
Where is waged the daily strife
With common wants and common cares
Which sows the human heart with tares—

70

' Lastly from the palaces
Where the murmur of distress
Echoes, like the distant sound
Of a wind alive around

71

' Those prison halls of wealth and fashion,
Where some few feel such compassion
For those who groan, and toil, and wail
As must make their brethren pale—

THE MASK OF ANARCHY

72

'Ye who suffer woes untold,
Or to feel, or to behold
Your lost country bought and sold
With a price of blood and gold—

73

'Let a vast assembly be,
And with great solemnity
Declare with measured words that ye
Are, as God has made ye, free—

74

'Be your strong and simple words
Keen to wound as sharpened swords,
And wide as targes let them be,
With their shade to cover ye.

75

'Let the tyrants pour around
With a quick and startling sound,
Like the loosening of a sea,
Troops of armed emblazonry.

76

'Let the charged artillery drive
Till the dead air seems alive

THE MASK OF ANARCHY

With the clash of clanging wheels,
And the tramp of horses' heels.

77

'Let the fixèd bayonet
Gleam with sharp desire to wet
Its bright point in English blood
Looking keen as one for food.

78

'Let the horsemen's scimitars
Wheel and flash, like sphereless stars
Thirsting to eclipse their burning
In a sea of death and mourning.

79

'Stand ye calm and resolute,
Like a forest close and mute,
With folded arms and looks which are
Weapons of unvanquished war,

80

'And let Panic, who outspeeds
The career of armèd steeds
Pass, a disregarded shade
Through your phalanx undismayed.

81

'Let the laws of your own land,
Good or ill, between ye stand
Hand to hand, and foot to foot,
Arbiters of the dispute,

82

'The old laws of England—they
Whose reverend heads with age are gray,
Children of a wiser day;
And whose solemn voice must be
Thine own echo—Liberty!

83

'On those who first should violate
Such sacred heralds in their state
Rest the blood that must ensue,
And it will not rest on you.

84

'And if then the tyrants dare
Let them ride among you there,
Slash, and stab, and maim, and hew,—
What they like, that let them do.

85

'With folded arms and steady eyes,
And little fear, and less surprise,

THE MASK OF ANARCHY

Look upon them as they slay
Till their rage has died away.

86

'Then they will return with shame
To the place from which they came,
And the blood thus shed will speak
In hot blushes on their cheek.

87

'Every woman in the land
Will point at them as they stand—
They will hardly dare to greet
Their acquaintance in the street.

88

'And the bold, true warriors
Who have hugged Danger in wars
Will turn to those who would be free,
Ashamed of such base company.

89

'And that slaughter to the Nation
Shall steam up like inspiration,
Eloquent, oracular;
A volcano heard afar.

90

'And these words shall then become
Like Oppression's thundered doom
Ringing through each heart and brain,
Heard again—again—again—

91

'Rise like Lions after slumber
In unvanquishable number—
Shake your chains to earth like dew
Which in sleep had fallen on you—
Ye are many—they are few.'

1819.

PETER BELL THE THIRD

by

MICHING MALLECHO, Esq.

Is it a party in a parlour,
Crammed just as they on earth were crammed,
Some sipping punch—some sipping tea;
But, as you by their faces see,
All silent, and all—damned!

'Peter Bell,' by W. Wordsworth.

OPHELIA.—What means this, my lord?
HAMLET.—Marry, this is Miching Mallecho; it means mischief.

Shakespeare.

*

DEDICATION

To Thomas Brown, Esq., The Younger, H.F.

DEAR TOM—Allow me to request you to intro-
duce Mr. Peter Bell to the respectable family of
the Fudges. Although he may fall short of those very
considerable personages in the more active properties
which characterize the Rat and the Apostate, I suspect
that even you, their historian, will confess that he sur-
passes them in the more peculiarly legitimate qualifi-
cation of intolerable dulness.

PETER BELL THE THIRD

You know Mr. Examiner Hunt; well—it was he who presented me to two of the Mr. Bells. My intimacy with the younger Mr. Bell naturally sprung from this intro-duction to his brothers. And in presenting him to you, I have the satisfaction of being able to assure you that he is considerably the dullest of the three.

There is this particular advantage in an acquaint-ance with any one of the Peter Bells, that if you know one Peter Bell, you know three Peter Bells; they are not one, but three; not three, but one. An awful mystery, which, after having caused torrents of blood, and having been hymned by groans enough to deafen the music of the spheres, is at length illustrated to the satisfaction of all parties in the theological world, by the nature of Mr. Peter Bell.

Peter is a polyhedric Peter, or a Peter with many sides. He changes colours like a chameleon, and his coat like a snake. He is a Proteus of a Peter. He was at first sublime, pathetic, impressive, profound; then dull; then prosy and dull; and now dull—oh so very dull! it is an ultra-legitimate dulness.

You will perceive that it is not necessary to consider Hell and the Devil as supernatural machinery. The whole scene of my epic is in 'this world which is'—so Peter informed us before his conversion to 'White Obi'—

134

PETER BELL THE THIRD

'The world of all of us, and where
We find our happiness, or not at all.'

Let me observe that I have spent six or seven days
in composing this sublime piece; the orb of my moon-
like genius has made the fourth part of its revolution
round the dull earth which you inhabit, driving you mad,
while it has retained its calmness and its splendour, and
I have been fitting this its last phase 'to occupy a per-
manent station in the literature of my country.'

Your works, indeed, dear Tom, sell better; but mine
are far superior. The public is no judge; posterity sets
all to rights.

Allow me to observe that so much has been written
of Peter Bell, that the present history can be considered
only, like the 'Iliad,' as a continuation of that series of
cyclic poems, which have already been candidates for
bestowing immortality upon, at the same time that they
receive it from, his character and adventures. In this
point of view I have violated no rule of syntax in begin-
ning my composition with a conjunction; the full stop
which closes the poem continued by me being, like the
full stops at the end of the 'Iliad' and 'Odyssey,' a full
stop of a very qualified import.

Hoping that the immortality which you have given
to the Fudges, you will receive from them; and in the

firm expectation, that when London shall be an habitation of bitterns; when St. Paul's and Westminster Abbey shall stand, shapeless and nameless ruins, in the midst of an unpeopled marsh; when the piers of Waterloo Bridge shall become the nuclei of islets of reeds and osiers, and cast the jagged shadows of their broken arches on the solitary stream, some transatlantic commentator will be weighing in the scales of some new and now unimagined system of criticism, the respective merits of the Bells and the Fudges, and their historians. I remain, dear Tom, yours sincerely,

Miching Mallecho.

December 1, 1819.

P.S. — Pray excuse the date of place; so soon as the profits of the publication come in, I mean to hire lodgings in a more respectable street.

PROLOGUE

PETER BELLS, one, two and three,
  O'er the wide world wandering be. —
First, the antenatal Peter,
Wrapped in weeds of the same metre,
The so-long-predestined raiment
Clothed in which to walk his way meant
The second Peter; whose ambition
Is to link the proposition,
As the mean of two extremes—
(This was learned from Aldric's themes)
Shielding from the guilt of schism
The orthodoxal syllogism;
The First Peter—he who was
Like the shadow in the glass
Of the second, yet unripe,
His substantial antitype. —
Then came Peter Bell the Second,
Who henceforward must be reckoned
The body of a double soul,
And that portion of the whole
Without which the rest would seem
Ends of a disjointed dream. —
And the Third is he who has

PETER BELL THE THIRD

O'er the grave been forced to pass
To the other side, which is, —
Go and try else, —just like this.

Peter Bell the First was Peter
Smugger, milder, softer, neater,
Like the soul before it is
Born from *that* world into *this*.
The next Peter Bell was he,
Predevote, like you and me,
To good or evil as may come;
His was the severer doom, —
For he was an evil Cotter,
And a polygamic Potter.[1]
And the last is Peter Bell,
Damned since our first parents fell,
Damned eternally to Hell—
Surely he deserves it well!

[1] The oldest scholiasts read—
       A *dodecagamic* Potter.
This is at once more descriptive and more megalo-
phonous, —but the alliteration of the text had capti-
vated the vulgar ear of the herd of later commentators.

PART THE FIRST

Death

1

AND Peter Bell, when he had been
With fresh-imported Hell-fire warmed,
Grew serious—from his dress and mien
'Twas very plainly to be seen
    Peter was quite reformed.

2

His eyes turned up, his mouth turned down;
    His accent caught a nasal twang;
He oiled his hair[1]; there might be heard
The grace of God in every word
    Which Peter said or sang.

---

[1] To those who have not duly appreciated the distinction between 'Whale' and 'Russia' oil, this attribute might rather seem to belong to the Dandy than the Evangelic. The effect, when to the windward, is indeed so similar, that it requires a subtle naturalist to discriminate the animals. They belong, however, to distinct genera.

PETER BELL THE THIRD

3

But Peter now grew old, and had
   An ill no doctor could unravel;
His torments almost drove him mad;—
Some said it was a fever bad—
   Some swore it was the gravel.

4

His holy friends then came about,
   And with long preaching and persuasion
Convinced the patient that, without
The smallest shadow of a doubt,
   He was predestined to damnation.

5

They said—'Thy name is Peter Bell;
   Thy skin is of a brimstone hue;
Alive or dead—ay, sick or well—
The one God made to rhyme with hell;
   The other, I think, rhymes with you.'

6

Then Peter set up such a yell!—
   The nurse, who with some water gruel
Was climbing up the stairs, as well
As her old legs could climb them—fell,
   And broke them both—the fall was cruel.

PETER BELL THE THIRD

7

The Parson from the casement lept
   Into the lake of Windermere—
And many an eel—though no adept
In God's right reason for it—kept
   Gnawing his kidneys half a year.

8

And all the rest rushed through the door,
   And tumbled over one another,
And broke their skulls.—Upon the floor
Meanwhile sat Peter Bell, and swore,
   And cursed his father and his mother;

9

And raved of God, and sin, and death,
   Blaspheming like an infidel;
And said, that with his clenchèd teeth
He'd seize the earth from underneath,
   And drag it with him down to hell.

10

As he was speaking came a spasm,
   And wrenched his gnashing teeth asunder;
Like one who sees a strange phantasm
He lay,—there was a silent chasm
   Between his upper jaw and under.

PETER BELL THE THIRD

11

And yellow death lay on his face;
   And a fixed smile that was not human
Told, as I understand the case,
That he was gone to the wrong place:—
   I heard all this from the old woman.

12

Then there came down from Langdale Pike
   A cloud, with lightning, wind and hail;
It swept over the mountains like
An ocean,—and I heard it strike
   The woods and crags of Grasmere vale.

13

And I saw the black storm come
   Nearer, minute after minute;
Its thunder made the cataracts dumb;
With hiss, and clash, and hollow hum,
   It neared as if the Devil was in it.

14

The Devil *was* in it:—he had bought
   Peter for half-a-crown; and when
The storm which bore him vanished, nought
That in the house that storm had caught
   Was ever seen again.

PETER BELL THE THIRD

15

The gaping neighbours came next day—
   They found all vanished from the shore:
The Bible, whence he used to pray,
Half scorched under a hen-coop lay;
   Smashed glass—and nothing more!

PART THE SECOND

The Devil

1

THE Devil, I safely can aver,
   Has neither hoof, nor tail, nor sting;
Nor is he, as some sages swear,
A spirit, neither here nor there,
   In nothing—yet in everything.

2

He is—what we are; for sometimes
   The Devil is a gentleman;
At others a bard bartering rhymes
For sack; a statesman spinning crimes;
   A swindler, living as he can;

3

A thief, who cometh in the night,
   With whole boots and net pantaloons,
Like some one whom it were not right
To mention;—or the luckless wight
   From whom he steals nine silver spoons.

4

But in this case he did appear
   Like a slop-merchant from Wapping,

144

PETER BELL THE THIRD

And with smug face, and eye severe,
On every side did perk and peer
   Till he saw Peter dead or napping.

5

He had on an upper Benjamin
   (For he was of the driving schism)
In the which he wrapped his skin
From the storm he travelled in,
   For fear of rheumatism.

He called the ghost out of the corse;—
   It was exceedingly like Peter,—
Only its voice was hollow and hoarse—
It had a queerish look of course—
   Its dress too was a little neater.

7

The Devil knew not his name and lot;
   Peter knew not that he was Bell:
Each had an upper stream of thought,
Which made all seem as it was not;
   Fitting itself to all things well.

8

Peter thought he had parents dear,
   Brothers, sisters, cousins, cronies,

PETER BELL THE THIRD

In the fens of Lincolnshire;
He perhaps had found them there
    Had he gone and boldly shown his

9

Solemn phiz in his own village;
    Where he thought oft when a boy
He'd clomb the orchard walls to pillage
The produce of his neighbour's tillage,
    With marvellous pride and joy.

10

And the Devil thought he had,
    'Mid the misery and confusion
Of an unjust war, just made
A fortune by the gainful trade
Of giving soldiers rations bad—
    The world is full of strange delusion—

11

That he had a mansion planned
    In a square like Grosvenor Square,
That he was aping fashion, and
That he now came to Westmoreland
    To see what was romantic there.

PETER BELL THE THIRD

12

And all this, though quite ideal, —
　Ready at a breath to vanish, —
Was a state not more unreal
Than the peace he could not feel,
　Or the care he could not banish.

13

After a little conversation,
　The Devil told Peter, if he chose,
He'd bring him to the world of fashion
By giving him a situation
　In his own service—and new clothes.

14

And Peter bowed, quite pleased and proud,
　And after waiting some few days
For a new livery—dirty yellow
Turned up with black—the wretched fellow
　Was bowled to Hell in the Devil's chaise.

PART THE THIRD
Hell

I

HELL is a city much like London—
  A populous and a smoky city;
There are all sorts of people undone,
And there is little or no fun done;
  Small justice shown, and still less pity.

2

There is a Castles, and a Canning,
  A Cobbett, and a Castlereagh;
All sorts of caitiff corpses planning
All sorts of cozening for trepanning
  Corpses less corrupt than they.

3

There is a * * * , who has lost
  His wits, or sold them, none knows which;
He walks about a double ghost,
And though as thin as Fraud almost—
  Ever grows more grim and rich.

4

There is a Chancery Court; a King;
  A manufacturing mob; a set

148

PETER BELL THE THIRD

Of thieves who by themselves are sent
Similar thieves to represent;
   An army; and a public debt.

5

Which last is a scheme of paper money,
   And means—being interpreted—
'Bees, keep your wax—give us the honey,
And we will plant, while skies are sunny,
   Flowers, which in winter serve instead.'

6

There is a great talk of revolution—
   And a great chance of despotism—
German soldiers—camps—confusion—
Tumults—lotteries—rage—delusion—
   Gin—suicide—and methodism;

7

Taxes too, on wine and bread,
   And meat, and beer, and tea, and cheese,
From which those patriots pure are fed,
Who gorge before they reel to bed
   The tenfold essence of all these.

8

There are mincing women, mewing,
  (Like cats, who *amant miserè*[1],)
Of their own virtue, and pursuing
Their gentler sisters to that ruin,
  Without which—what were chastity?[2]

9

Lawyers—judges—old hobnobbers
  Are there—bailiffs—chancellors—
Bishops—great and little robbers—

[1] One of the attributes in Linnaeus's description of the Cat. To a similar cause the caterwauling of more than one species of this genus is to be referred;—except, indeed, that the poor quadruped is compelled to quarrel with its own pleasures, whilst the biped is supposed only to quarrel with those of others.

[2] What would this husk and excuse for a virtue be without its kernel prostitution, or the kernel prostitution without this husk of a virtue? I wonder the women of the town do not form an association, like the Society for the Suppression of Vice, for the support of what may be called the 'King, Church, and Constitution' of their order. But this subject is almost too horrible for a joke.

PETER BELL THE THIRD

Rhymesters—pamphleteers—stock-jobbers—
Men of glory in the wars,—

10

Things whose trade is, over ladies
   To lean, and flirt, and stare, and simper,
Till all that is divine in woman
Grows cruel, courteous, smooth, inhuman,
   Crucified 'twixt a smile and whimper.

11

Thrusting, toiling, wailing, moiling,
   Frowning, preaching—such a riot!
Each with never-ceasing labour,
Whilst he thinks he cheats his neighbour,
   Cheating his own heart of quiet.

12

And all these meet at levees;—
   Dinners convivial and political;—
Suppers of epic poets;—teas,
Where small talk dies in agonies;—
   Breakfasts professional and critical;

13

Lunches and snacks so aldermanic
   That one would furnish forth ten dinners,

PETER BELL THE THIRD

Where reigns a Cretan-tonguèd panic,
Lest news Russ, Dutch, or Alemannic
　Should make some losers, and some winners;—

14

At conversazioni—balls—
　Conventicles—and drawing-rooms—
Courts of law—committees—calls
Of a morning—clubs—book-stalls—
　Churches—masquerades—and tombs.

15

And this is Hell—and in this smother
　All are damnable and damned;
Each one damning, damns the other;
They are damned by one another,
　By none other are they damned.

16

'Tis a lie to say, 'God damns[1]!'
　Where was Heaven's Attorney General
When they first gave out such flams?

---

[1] This libel on our national oath, and this accusation of all our countrymen of being in the daily practice of solemnly asseverating the most enormous falsehood, I fear deserves the notice of a more active Attorney General than that here alluded to.

PETER BELL THE THIRD

Let there be an end of shams,
  They are mines of poisonous mineral.

17

Statesmen damn themselves to be
  Cursed; and lawyers damn their souls
To the auction of a fee;
Churchmen damn themselves to see
  God's sweet love in burning coals.

18

The rich are damned, beyond all cure,
  To taunt, and starve, and trample on
The weak and wretched; and the poor
Damn their broken hearts to endure
  Stripe on stripe, with groan on groan.

19

Sometimes the poor are damned indeed
  To take,—not means for being blessed,—
But Cobbett's snuff, revenge; that weed
From which the worms that it doth feed
  Squeeze less than they before possessed.

20

And some few, like we know who,
  Damned—but God alone knows why—

PETER BELL THE THIRD

To believe their minds are given
To make this ugly Hell a Heaven;
   In which faith they live and die.

21

Thus, as in a town, plague-stricken,
   Each man be he sound or no
Must indifferently sicken;
As when day begins to thicken,
   None knows a pigeon from a crow, —

22

So good and bad, sane and mad,
   The oppressor and the oppressed;
Those who weep to see what others
Smile to inflict upon their brothers;
   Lovers, haters, worst and best;

23

All are damned—they breathe an air,
   Thick, infected, joy-dispelling:
Each pursues what seems most fair,
Mining like moles, through mind, and there
Scoop palace-caverns vast, where Care
   In thronèd state is ever dwelling.

PART THE FOURTH

Sin

1

LO, Peter in Hell's Grosvenor Square,
  A footman in the Devil's service!
And the misjudging world would swear
That every man in service there
  To virtue would prefer vice.

2

But Peter, though now damned, was not
  What Peter was before damnation.
Men oftentimes prepare a lot
Which ere it finds them, is not what
  Suits with their genuine station.

3

All things that Peter saw and felt
  Had a peculiar aspect to him;
And when they came within the belt
Of his own nature, seemed to melt,
  Like cloud to cloud, into him.

4

And so the outward world uniting
  To that within him, he became

PETER BELL THE THIRD

Considerably uninviting
To those who, meditation slighting,
   Were moulded in a different frame.

5

And he scorned them, and they scorned him;
   And he scorned all they did; and they
Did all that men of their own trim
Are wont to do to please their whim,
   Drinking, lying, swearing, play.

6

Such were his fellow-servants; thus
   His virtue, like our own, was built
Too much on that indignant fuss
Hypocrite Pride stirs up in us
   To bully one another's guilt.

7

He had a mind which was somehow
   At once circumference and centre
Of all he might or feel or know;
Nothing went ever out, although
   Something did ever enter.

8

He had as much imagination
   As a pint-pot;—he never could

PETER BELL THE THIRD

Fancy another situation,
From which to dart his contemplation,
  Than that wherein he stood.

9

Yet his was individual mind,
  And new created all he saw
In a new manner, and refined
Those new creations, and combined
  Them, by a master-spirit's law.

10

Thus—though unimaginative—
  An apprehension clear, intense,
Of his mind's work, had made alive
The things it wrought on; I believe
  Wakening a sort of thought in sense.

11

But from the first 'twas Peter's drift
  To be a kind of moral eunuch,
He touched the hem of Nature's shift,
Felt faint—and never dared uplift
  The closest, all-concealing tunic.

12

She laughed the while, with an arch smile,
  And kissed him with a sister's kiss,

PETER BELL THE THIRD

And said—' My best Diogenes,
I love you well—but, if you please,
   Tempt not again my deepest bliss.

13

' 'Tis you are cold—for I, not coy,
   Yield love for love, frank, warm, and true;
And Burns, a Scottish peasant boy—
His errors prove it—knew my joy
   More, learnèd friend, than you.

14

' *Bocca bacciata non perde ventura,*
   Anzi rinnuova come fa la luna:—
So thought Boccaccio, whose sweet words might cure a
Male prude, like you, from what you now endure, a
   Low-tide in soul, like a stagnant laguna.'

15

Then Peter rubbed his eyes severe,
   And smoothed his spacious forehead down
With his broad palm;—'twixt love and fear,
He looked, as he no doubt felt, queer,
   And in his dream sate down.

16

The Devil was no uncommon creature;
   A leaden-witted thief—just huddled

PETER BELL THE THIRD

Out of the dross and scum of nature;
A toad-like lump of limb and feature,
   With mind, and heart, and fancy muddled.

17

He was that heavy, dull, cold thing,
   The spirit of evil well may be:
A drone too base to have a sting;
Who gluts, and grimes his lazy wing,
   And calls lust, luxury.

18

Now he was quite the kind of wight
   Round whom collect, at a fixed aera,
Venison, turtle, hock, and claret, —
Good cheer—and those who come to share it—
   And best East Indian madeira!

19

It was his fancy to invite
   Men of science, wit, and learning,
Who came to lend each other light;
He proudly thought that his gold's might
   Had set those spirits burning.

20

And men of learning, science, wit,
   Considered him as you and I

PETER BELL THE THIRD

Think of some rotten tree, and sit
Lounging and dining under it,
  Exposed to the wide sky.

21

And all the while, with loose fat smile,
  The willing wretch sat winking there,
Believing 'twas his power that made
That jovial scene—and that all paid
  Homage to his unnoticed chair.

22

Though to be sure this place was Hell;
  He was the Devil—and all they—
What though the claret circled well,
And wit, like ocean, rose and fell?—
  Were damned eternally.

PART THE FIFTH
Grace

1

AMONG the guests who often stayed
   Till the Devil's petits-soupers,
A man there came, fair as a maid,
And Peter noted what he said,
   Standing behind his master's chair.

2

He was a mighty poet—and
   A subtle-souled psychologist;
All things he seemed to understand,
Of old or new—of sea or land—
   But his own mind—which was a mist.

3

This was a man who might have turned
   Hell into Heaven—and so in gladness
A Heaven unto himself have earned;
But he in shadows undiscerned
   Trusted,—and damned himself to madness.

4

He spoke of poetry, and how
   'Divine it was—a light—a love—

PETER BELL THE THIRD

A spirit which like wind doth blow
As it listeth, to and fro;
  A dew rained down from God above;

5

'A power which comes and goes like dream,
  And which none can ever trace—
Heaven's light on earth—Truth's brightest beam.'
And when he ceased there lay the gleam
  Of those words upon his face.

6

Now Peter, when he heard such talk,
  Would, heedless of a broken pate,
Stand like a man asleep, or balk
Some wishing guest of knife or fork,
  Or drop and break his master's plate.

7

At night he oft would start and wake
  Like a lover, and began
In a wild measure songs to make
On moor, and glen, and rocky lake,
  And on the heart of man—

8

And on the universal sky—
  And the wide earth's bosom green,—

PETER BELL THE THIRD

And the sweet, strange mystery
Of what beyond these things may lie,
   And yet remain unseen.

9

For in his thought he visited
   The spots in which, ere dead and damned,
He his wayward life had led;
Yet knew not whence the thoughts were fed
   Which thus his fancy crammed.

10

And these obscure remembrances
   Stirred such harmony in Peter,
That, whensoever he should please,
He could speak of rocks and trees
   In poetic metre.

11

For though it was without a sense
   Of memory, yet he remembered well
Many a ditch and quick-set fence;
Of lakes he had intelligence,
   He knew something of heath and fell.

12

He had also dim recollections
   Of pedlars tramping on their rounds;

Milk-pans and pails; and odd collections
Of saws, and proverbs; and reflections
   Old parsons make in burying-grounds.

13

But Peter's verse was clear, and came
   Announcing from the frozen hearth
Of a cold age, that none might tame
The soul of that diviner flame
   It augured to the Earth:

14

Like gentle rains, on the dry plains,
   Making that green which late was gray,
Or like the sudden moon, that stains
Some gloomy chamber's window-panes
   With a broad light like day.

15

For language was in Peter's hand
   Like clay while he was yet a potter;
And he made songs for all the land,
Sweet both to feel and understand,
   As pipkins late to mountain Cotter.

16

And Mr. —, the bookseller,
   Gave twenty pounds for some;—then scorning

PETER BELL THE THIRD

A footman's yellow coat to wear,
Peter, too proud of heart, I fear,
   Instantly gave the Devil warning.

17

Whereat the Devil took offence,
   And swore in his soul a great oath then,
'That for his damned impertinence
He'd bring him to a proper sense
   Of what was due to gentlemen!'

PART THE SIXTH
Damnation

1

'O that mine enemy had written
    A book!'—cried Job:—a fearful curse,
If to the Arab, as the Briton,
'Twas galling to be critic-bitten:—
    The Devil to Peter wished no worse.

2

When Peter's next new book found vent,
    The Devil to all the first Reviews
A copy of it slyly sent,
With five-pound note as compliment,
    And this short notice—'Pray abuse.'

3

Then *seriatim*, month and quarter,
    Appeared such mad tirades. —One said—
'Peter seduced Mrs. Foy's daughter,
Then drowned the mother in Ullswater,
    The last thing as he went to bed.'

4

Another—'Let him shave his head!
    Where's Dr. Willis?—Or is he joking?

PETER BELL THE THIRD

What does the rascal mean or hope,
No longer imitating Pope,
   In that barbarian Shakespeare poking?'

5

One more, 'Is incest not enough?
   And must there be adultery too?
Grace after meat? Miscreant and Liar!
Thief! Blackguard! Scoundrel! Fool! Hell-fire
   Is twenty times too good for you.

6

'By that last book of yours WE think
   You've double damned yourself to scorn;
We warned you whilst yet on the brink
You stood. From your black name will shrink
   The babe that is unborn.'

7

All these Reviews the Devil made
   Up in a parcel, which he had
Safely to Peter's house conveyed.
For carriage, tenpence Peter paid—
   Untied them—read them—went half mad.

8

'What!' cried he, 'this is my reward
   For nights of thought, and days of toil?

167

PETER BELL THE THIRD

Do poets, but to be abhorred
By men of whom they never heard,
   Consume their spirits' oil?

9

'What have I done to them?—and who
   Is Mrs. Foy? 'Tis very cruel
To speak of me and Betty so!
Adultery! God defend me! Oh!
   I've half a mind to fight a duel.

10

'Or,' cried he, a grave look collecting,
   'Is it my genius, like the moon,
Sets those who stand her face inspecting,
That face within their brain reflecting,
   Like a crazed bell-chime, out of tune?'

11

For Peter did not know the town,
   But thought, as country readers do,
For half a guinea or a crown,
He bought oblivion or renown
   From God's own voice[1] in a review.

[1] *Vox populi, vox dei.* As Mr. Godwin truly observes of a more famous saying, 'of some merit as a popular maxim, but totally destitute of philosophical accuracy.'

PETER BELL THE THIRD

12

All Peter did on this occasion
    Was, writing some sad stuff in prose.
It is a dangerous invasion
When poets criticize; their station
    Is to delight, not pose.

13

The Devil then sent to Leipsic fair
    For Born's translation of Kant's book;
A world of words, tail foremost, where
Right—wrong—false—true—and foul—and fair
    As in a lottery-wheel are shook.

14

Five thousand crammed octavo pages
    Of German psychologics,—he
Who his *furor verborum* assuages
Thereon, deserves just seven months' wages
    More than will e'er be due to me.

15

I looked on them nine several days,
    And then I saw that they were bad;
A friend, too, spoke in their dispraise, —
He never read them;—with amaze
    I found Sir William Drummond had.

16

When the book came, the Devil sent
    It to P. Verbovale[1], Esquire,
With a brief note of compliment,
By that night's Carlisle mail. It went,
    And set his soul on fire.

17

Fire, which *ex luce praebens fumum*,
    Made him beyond the bottom see
Of truth's clear well—when I and you, Ma'am,
Go, as we shall do, *subter humum*,
    We may know more than he.

18

Now Peter ran to seed in soul
    Into a walking paradox;
For he was neither part nor whole,
Nor good, nor bad—nor knave nor fool;
    —Among the woods and rocks.

[1] Quasi, *Qui valet verba*:—i.e. all the words which have been, are, or may be expended by, for, against, with, or on him. A sufficient proof of the utility of this history. Peter's progenitor who selected this name seems to have possessed 'a pure anticipated cognition' of the nature and modesty of this ornament of his posterity.

PETER BELL THE THIRD

19

Furious he rode, where late he ran,
   Lashing and spurring his tame hobby;
Turned to a formal puritan,
A solemn and unsexual man, —
   He half believed 'White Obi.'

20

This steed in vision he would ride,
   High trotting over nine-inch bridges,
With Flibbertigibbet, imp of pride,
Mocking and mowing by his side —
A mad-brained goblin for a guide —
   Over corn-fields, gates, and hedges.

21

After these ghastly rides, he came
   Home to his heart, and found from thence
Much stolen of its accustomed flame;
His thoughts grew weak, drowsy, and lame
   Of their intelligence.

22

To Peter's view, all seemed one hue;
   He was no Whig, he was no Tory;
No Deist and no Christian he; —

PETER BELL THE THIRD

He got so subtle, that to be
    Nothing, was all his glory.

23

One single point in his belief
    From his organization sprung,
The heart-enrooted faith, the chief
Ear in his doctrines' blighted sheaf,
    That 'Happiness is wrong';

24

So thought Calvin and Dominic;
    So think their fierce successors, who
Even now would neither stint nor stick
Our flesh from off our bones to pick,
    If they might 'do their do.'

25

His morals thus were undermined:—
    The old Peter—the hard, old Potter—
Was born anew within his mind;
He grew dull, harsh, sly, unrefined,
    As when he tramped beside the Otter[1].

[1] A famous river in the new Atlantis of the Dynasto-
phylic Pantisocratists.

PETER BELL THE THIRD

26

In the death hues of agony
    Lambently flashing from a fish,
Now Peter felt amused to see
Shades like a rainbow's rise and flee,
    Mixed with a certain hungry wish[1].

27

So in his Country's dying face
    He looked—and, lovely as she lay,

[1] See the description of the beautiful colours produced during the agonizing death of a number of trout, in the fourth part of a long poem in blank verse, published within a few years. ['The Excursion,' VIII. ll. 568-71.—Ed.] That poem contains curious evidence of the gradual hardening of a strong but circumscribed sensibility, of the perversion of a penetrating but panic-stricken understanding. The author might have derived a lesson which he had probably forgotten from these sweet and sublime verses:—

'This lesson, Shepherd, let us two divide,
  Taught both by what she* shows and what conceals,
Never to blend our pleasure or our pride
With sorrow of the meanest thing that feels.'
          * Nature.

PETER BELL THE THIRD

Seeking in vain his last embrace,
Wailing her own abandoned case,
 With hardened sneer he turned away:

28

And coolly to his own soul said;—
 'Do you not think that we might make
A poem on her when she's dead:—
Or, no—a thought is in my head—
 Her shroud for a new sheet I'll take:

29

'My wife wants one.—Let who will bury
 This mangled corpse! And I and you,
My dearest Soul, will then make merry,
As the Prince Regent did with Sherry,—'
 'Ay—and at last desert me too.'

30

And so his Soul would not be gay,
 But moaned within him; like a fawn
Moaning within a cave, it lay
Wounded and wasting, day by day,
 Till all its life of life was gone.

31

As troubled skies stain waters clear,
 The storm in Peter's heart and mind

PETER BELL THE THIRD

Now made his verses dark and queer:
They were the ghosts of what they were,
   Shaking dim grave-clothes in the wind.

32

For he now raved enormous folly,
   Of Baptisms, Sunday-schools, and Graves,
'Twould make George Colman melancholy
To have heard him, like a male Molly,
   Chanting those stupid staves.

33

Yet the Reviews, who heaped abuse
   On Peter while he wrote for freedom,
So soon as in his song they spy
The folly which soothes tyranny,
   Praise him, for those who feed 'em.

34

' He was a man, too great to scan;—
   A planet lost in truth's keen rays:—
His virtue, awful and prodigious;—
He was the most sublime, religious,
   Pure-minded Poet of these days.'

35

As soon as he read that, cried Peter,
   'Eureka! I have found the way

PETER BELL THE THIRD

To make a better thing of metre
Than e'er was made by living creature
  Up to this blessèd day.'

36

Then Peter wrote odes to the Devil;—
  In one of which he meekly said:
'May Carnage and Slaughter,
Thy niece and thy daughter,
May Rapine and Famine,
Thy gorge ever cramming,
  Glut thee with living and dead!

37

'May Death and Damnation,
  And Consternation,
Flit up from Hell with pure intent!
  Slash them at Manchester,
  Glasgow, Leeds, and Chester;
Drench all with blood from Avon to Trent.

38

'Let thy body-guard yeomen
Hew down babes and women,
And laugh with bold triumph till Heaven be rent!

PETER BELL THE THIRD

When Moloch in Jewry
Munched children with fury,
It was thou, Devil, dining with pure intent [1].'

[1] It is curious to observe how often extremes meet.
Cobbett and Peter use the same language for a different
purpose: Peter is indeed a sort of metrical Cobbett.
Cobbett is, however, more mischievous than Peter,
because he pollutes a holy and now unconquerable
cause with the principles of legitimate murder; whilst
the other only makes a bad one ridiculous and odious.

If either Peter or Cobbett should see this note, each
will feel more indignation at being compared to the
other than at any censure implied in the moral per-
version laid to their charge.

PART THE SEVENTH

Double Damnation

1

THE Devil now knew his proper cue.—
  Soon as he read the ode, he drove
To his friend Lord MacMurderchouse's,
A man of interest in both houses,
  And said:—'For money or for love,

2

'Pray find some cure or sinecure;
  To feed from the superfluous taxes
A friend of ours—a poet—fewer
Have fluttered tamer to the lure
  Than he.' His lordship stands and racks his

3

Stupid brains, while one might count
  As many beads as he had boroughs,—
At length replies; from his mean front,
Like one who rubs out an account,
  Smoothing away the unmeaning furrows:

4

'It happens fortunately, dear Sir,
  I can. I hope I need require

PETER BELL THE THIRD

No pledge from you, that he will stir
In our affairs; like Oliver,
   That he'll be worthy of his hire.'

5

These words exchanged, the news sent off
   To Peter, home the Devil hied, —
Took to his bed; he had no cough,
No doctor, — meat and drink enough, —
   Yet that same night he died.

6

The Devil's corpse was leaded down;
   His decent heirs enjoyed his pelf,
Mourning-coaches, many a one,
Followed his hearse along the town: —
   Where was the Devil himself?

7

When Peter heard of his promotion,
   His eyes grew like two stars for bliss:
There was a bow of sleek devotion
Engendering in his back; each motion
   Seemed a Lord's shoe to kiss.

8

He hired a house, bought plate, and made
   A genteel drive up to his door,

PETER BELL THE THIRD

With sifted gravel neatly laid, —
As if defying all who said,
   Peter was ever poor.

9

But a disease soon struck into
   The very life and soul of Peter—
He walked about—slept—had the hue
Of health upon his cheeks—and few
   Dug better—none a heartier eater.

10

And yet a strange and horrid curse
   Clung upon Peter, night and day;
Month after month the thing grew worse,
And deadlier than in this my verse
   I can find strength to say.

11

Peter was dull—he was at first
   Dull—oh, so dull—so very dull!
Whether he talked, wrote, or rehearsed—
Still with this dulness was he cursed—
   Dull—beyond all conception—dull.

12

No one could read his books—no mortal,
   But a few natural friends, would hear him;

PETER BELL THE THIRD

The parson came not near his portal;
His state was like that of the immortal
   Described by Swift—no man could bear him.

13

His sister, wife, and children yawned,
   With a long, slow, and drear ennui,
All human patience far beyond;
Their hopes of Heaven each would have pawned,
   Anywhere else to be.

14

But in his verse, and in his prose,
   The essence of his dulness was
Concentred and compressed so close,
'Twould have made Guatimozin doze
   On his red gridiron of brass.

15

A printer's boy, folding those pages,
   Fell slumbrously upon one side;
Like those famed Seven who slept three ages.
To wakeful frenzy's vigil-rages,
   As opiates, were the same applied.

16

Even the Reviewers who were hired
   To do the work of his reviewing,

PETER BELL THE THIRD

With adamantine nerves, grew tired;—
Gaping and torpid they retired,
   To dream of what they should be doing.

17

And worse and worse, the drowsy curse
   Yawned in him, till it grew a pest—
A wide contagious atmosphere,
Creeping like cold through all things near;
   A power to infect and to infest.

18

His servant-maids and dogs grew dull;
   His kitten, late a sportive elf;
The woods and lakes, so beautiful,
Of dim stupidity were full,
   All grew dull as Peter's self.

19

The earth under his feet—the springs,
   Which lived within it a quick life,
The air, the winds of many wings,
That fan it with new murmurings,
   Were dead to their harmonious strife.

20

The birds and beasts within the wood,
   The insects, and each creeping thing,

PETER BELL THE THIRD

Were now a silent multitude;
Love's work was left unwrought—no brood
  Near Peter's house took wing.

21

And every neighbouring cottager
  Stupidly yawned upon the other:
No jackass brayed; no little cur
Cocked up his ears;—no man would stir
  To save a dying mother.

22

Yet all from that charmed district went
  But some half-idiot and half-knave,
Who rather than pay any rent,
Would live with marvellous content,
  Over his father's grave.

23

No bailiff dared within that space,
  For fear of the dull charm, to enter;
A man would bear upon his face,
For fifteen months in any case,
  The yawn of such a venture.

PETER BELL THE THIRD

24

Seven miles above—below—around—
  This pest of dulness holds its sway;
A ghastly life without a sound;
To Peter's soul the spell is bound—
  How should it ever pass away?

1819.

THE SENSITIVE PLANT

PART FIRST

A SENSITIVE Plant in a garden grew,
 And the young winds fed it with silver dew,
And it opened its fan-like leaves to the light,
And closed them beneath the kisses of Night.

And the Spring arose on the garden fair,
Like the Spirit of Love felt everywhere;
And each flower and herb on Earth's dark breast
Rose from the dreams of its wintry rest.

But none ever trembled and panted with bliss
In the garden, the field, or the wilderness,
Like a doe in the noontide with love's sweet want,
As the companionless Sensitive Plant.

The snowdrop, and then the violet,
Arose from the ground with warm rain wet,
And their breath was mixed with fresh odour, sent
From the turf, like the voice and the instrument.

Then the pied wind-flowers and the tulip tall,
And narcissi, the fairest among them all,
Who gaze on their eyes in the stream's recess,
Till they die of their own dear loveliness;

THE SENSITIVE PLANT

And the Naiad-like lily of the vale,
Whom youth makes so fair and passion so pale
That the light of its tremulous bells is seen
Through their pavilions of tender green;

And the hyacinth purple, and white, and blue,
Which flung from its bells a sweet peal anew
Of music so delicate, soft, and intense,
It was felt like an odour within the sense;

And the rose like a nymph to the bath addressed,
Which unveiled the depth of her glowing breast,
Till, fold after fold, to the fainting air
The soul of her beauty and love lay bare:

And the wand-like lily, which lifted up,
As a Maenad, its moonlight-coloured cup,
Till the fiery star, which is its eye,
Gazed through clear dew on the tender sky;

And the jessamine faint, and the sweet tuberose,
The sweetest flower for scent that blows;
And all rare blossoms from every clime
Grew in that garden in perfect prime.

And on the stream whose inconstant bosom
Was pranked, under boughs of embowering blossom,
With golden and green light, slanting through
Their heaven of many a tangled hue,

THE SENSITIVE PLANT

Broad water-lilies lay tremulously,
And starry river-buds glimmered by,
And around them the soft stream did glide and dance
With a motion of sweet sound and radiance.

And the sinuous paths of lawn and of moss,
Which led through the garden along and across,
Some open at once to the sun and the breeze,
Some lost among bowers of blossoming trees,

Were all paved with daisies and delicate bells
As fair as the fabulous asphodels,
And flow'rets which, drooping as day drooped too,
Fell into pavilions, white, purple, and blue,
To roof the glow-worm from the evening dew.

And from this undefilèd Paradise
The flowers (as an infant's awakening eyes
Smile on its mother, whose singing sweet
Can first lull, and at last must awaken it),

When Heaven's blithe winds had unfolded them,
As mine-lamps enkindle a hidden gem,
Shone smiling to Heaven, and every one
Shared joy in the light of the gentle sun;

For each one was interpenetrated
With the light and the odour its neighbour shed,

THE SENSITIVE PLANT

Like young lovers whom youth and love make dear
Wrapped and filled by their mutual atmosphere.

But the Sensitive Plant which could give small fruit
Of the love which it felt from the leaf to the root,
Received more than all, it loved more than ever,
Where none wanted but it, could belong to the giver, —

For the Sensitive Plant has no bright flower;
Radiance and odour are not its dower;
It loves, even like Love, its deep heart is full,
It desires what it has not, the Beautiful!

The light winds which from unsustaining wings
Shed the music of many murmurings;
The beams which dart from many a star
Of the flowers whose hues they bear afar;

The plumèd insects swift and free,
Like golden boats on a sunny sea,
Laden with light and odour, which pass
Over the gleam of the living grass;

The unseen clouds of the dew, which lie
Like fire in the flowers till the sun rides high,
Then wander like spirits among the spheres,
Each cloud faint with the fragrance it bears;

The quivering vapours of dim noontide,
Which like a sea o'er the warm earth glide,

188

THE SENSITIVE PLANT

In which every sound, and odour, and beam,
Move, as reeds in a single stream;

Each and all like ministering angels were
For the Sensitive Plant sweet joy to bear,
Whilst the lagging hours of the day went by
Like windless clouds o'er a tender sky.

And when evening descended from Heaven above,
And the Earth was all rest, and the air was all love,
And delight, though less bright, was far more deep,
And the day's veil fell from the world of sleep,

And the beasts, and the birds, and the insects were drowned
In an ocean of dreams without a sound;
Whose waves never mark, though they ever impress
The light sand which paves it, consciousness;

(Only overhead the sweet nightingale
Ever sang more sweet as the day might fail,
And snatches of its Elysian chant
Were mixed with the dreams of the Sensitive Plant);—

The Sensitive Plant was the earliest
Upgathered into the bosom of rest;
A sweet child weary of its delight,
The feeblest and yet the favourite,
Cradled within the embrace of Night.

PART SECOND

THERE was a Power in this sweet place,
  An Eve in this Eden; a ruling Grace
Which to the flowers, did they waken or dream,
Was as God is to the starry scheme.

A Lady, the wonder of her kind,
Whose form was upborne by a lovely mind
Which, dilating, had moulded her mien and motion
Like a sea-flower unfolded beneath the ocean,

Tended the garden from morn to even:
And the meteors of that sublunar Heaven,
Like the lamps of the air when Night walks forth,
Laughed round her footsteps up from the Earth!

She had no companion of mortal race,
But her tremulous breath and her flushing face
Told, whilst the morn kissed the sleep from her eyes,
That her dreams were less slumber than Paradise:

As if some bright Spirit for her sweet sake
Had deserted Heaven while the stars were awake,
As if yet around her he lingering were,
Though the veil of daylight concealed him from her.

THE SENSITIVE PLANT

Her step seemed to pity the grass it pressed;
You might hear by the heaving of her breast,
That the coming and going of the wind
Brought pleasure there and left passion behind.

And wherever her aëry footstep trod,
Her trailing hair from the grassy sod
Erased its light vestige, with shadowy sweep,
Like a sunny storm o'er the dark green deep.

I doubt not the flowers of that garden sweet
Rejoiced in the sound of her gentle feet;
I doubt not they felt the spirit that came
From her glowing fingers through all her frame.

She sprinkled bright water from the stream
On those that were faint with the sunny beam;
And out of the cups of the heavy flowers
She emptied the rain of the thunder-showers.

She lifted their heads with her tender hands,
And sustained them with rods and osier-bands;
If the flowers had been her own infants, she
Could never have nursed them more tenderly.

And all killing insects and gnawing worms,
And things of obscene and unlovely forms,
She bore, in a basket of Indian woof,
Into the rough woods far aloof, —

THE SENSITIVE PLANT

In a basket, of grasses and wild-flowers full,
The freshest her gentle hands could pull
For the poor banished insects, whose intent,
Although they did ill, was innocent.

But the bee and the beamlike ephemeris
Whose path is the lightning's, and soft moths that kiss
The sweet lips of the flowers, and harm not, did she
Make her attendant angels be.

And many an antenatal tomb,
Where butterflies dream of the life to come,
She left clinging round the smooth and dark
Edge of the odorous cedar bark.

This fairest creature from earliest Spring
Thus moved through the garden ministering
All the sweet season of Summertide,
And ere the first leaf looked brown—she died!

PART THIRD

THREE days the flowers of the garden fair,
  Like stars when the moon is awakened, were,
Or the waves of Baiae, ere luminous
She floats up through the smoke of Vesuvius.

And on the fourth, the Sensitive Plant
Felt the sound of the funeral chant,
And the steps of the bearers, heavy and slow,
And the sobs of the mourners, deep and low;

The weary sound and the heavy breath,
And the silent motions of passing death,
And the smell, cold, oppressive, and dank,
Sent through the pores of the coffin-plank;

The dark grass, and the flowers among the grass,
Were bright with tears as the crowd did pass;
From their sighs the wind caught a mournful tone,
And sate in the pines, and gave groan for groan.

The garden, once fair, became cold and foul,
Like the corpse of her who had been its soul,
Which at first was lovely as if in sleep,
Then slowly changed, till it grew a heap
To make men tremble who never weep.

THE SENSITIVE PLANT

Swift Summer into the Autumn flowed,
And frost in the mist of the morning rode,
Though the noonday sun looked clear and bright,
Mocking the spoil of the secret night.

The rose-leaves, like flakes of crimson snow,
Paved the turf and the moss below.
The lilies were drooping, and white, and wan,
Like the head and the skin of a dying man.

And Indian plants, of scent and hue
The sweetest that ever were fed on dew,
Leaf by leaf, day after day,
Were massed into the common clay.

And the leaves, brown, yellow, and gray, and red,
And white with the whiteness of what is dead,
Like troops of ghosts on the dry wind passed;
Their whistling noise made the birds aghast.

And the gusty winds waked the wingèd seeds,
Out of their birthplace of ugly weeds,
Till they clung round many a sweet flower's stem,
Which rotted into the earth with them.

The water-blooms under the rivulet
Fell from the stalks on which they were set;
And the eddies drove them here and there,
As the winds did those of the upper air.

THE SENSITIVE PLANT

Then the rain came down, and the broken stalks
Were bent and tangled across the walks;
And the leafless network of parasite bowers
Massed into ruin; and all sweet flowers.

Between the time of the wind and the snow
All loathliest weeds began to grow,
Whose coarse leaves were splashed with many a speck,
Like the water-snake's belly and the toad's back.

And thistles, and nettles, and darnels rank,
And the dock, and henbane, and hemlock dank,
Stretched out its long and hollow shank,
And stifled the air till the dead wind stank.

And plants, at whose names the verse feels loath,
Filled the place with a monstrous undergrowth,
Prickly, and pulpous, and blistering, and blue,
Livid, and starred with a lurid dew.

And agarics, and fungi, with mildew and mould
Started like mist from the wet ground cold;
Pale, fleshy, as if the decaying dead
With a spirit of growth had been animated!

Spawn, weeds, and filth, a leprous scum,
Made the running rivulet thick and dumb,
And at its outlet flags huge as stakes
Dammed it up with roots knotted like water-snakes.

THE SENSITIVE PLANT

And hour by hour, when the air was still,
The vapours arose which have strength to kill;
At morn they were seen, at noon they were felt,
At night they were darkness no star could melt.

And unctuous meteors from spray to spray
Crept and flitted in broad noonday
Unseen; every branch on which they alit
By a venomous blight was burned and bit.

The Sensitive Plant, like one forbid,
Wept, and the tears within each lid
Of its folded leaves, which together grew,
Were changed to a blight of frozen glue.

For the leaves soon fell, and the branches soon
By the heavy axe of the blast were hewn;
The sap shrank to the root through every pore
As blood to a heart that will beat no more.

For Winter came: the wind was his whip:
One choppy finger was on his lip:
He had torn the cataracts from the hills
And they clanked at his girdle like manacles;

His breath was a chain which without a sound
The earth, and the air, and the water bound;
He came, fiercely driven, in his chariot-throne
By the tenfold blasts of the Arctic zone.

196

THE SENSITIVE PLANT

Then the weeds which were forms of living death
Fled from the frost to the earth beneath.
Their decay and sudden flight from frost
Was but like the vanishing of a ghost!

And under the roots of the Sensitive Plant
The moles and the dormice died for want:
The birds dropped stiff from the frozen air
And were caught in the branches naked and bare.

First there came down a thawing rain
And its dull drops froze on the boughs again;
Then there steamed up a freezing dew
Which to the drops of the thaw-rain grew;

And a northern whirlwind, wandering about
Like a wolf that had smelt a dead child out,
Shook the boughs thus laden, and heavy, and stiff,
And snapped them off with his rigid griff.

When Winter had gone and Spring came back
The Sensitive Plant was a leafless wreck;
But the mandrakes, and toadstools, and docks, and darnels,
Rose like the dead from their ruined charnels.

CONCLUSION

WHETHER the Sensitive Plant, or that
Which within its boughs like a Spirit sat,
Ere its outward form had known decay,
Now felt this change, I cannot say.

Whether that Lady's gentle mind,
No longer with the form combined
Which scattered love, as stars do light,
Found sadness, where it left delight,

I dare not guess; but in this life
Of error, ignorance, and strife,
Where nothing is, but all things seem,
And we the shadows of the dream,

It is a modest creed, and yet
Pleasant if one considers it,
To own that death itself must be,
Like all the rest, a mockery.

That garden sweet, that lady fair,
And all sweet shapes and odours there,
In truth have never passed away:
'Tis we, 'tis ours, are changed; not they.

THE SENSITIVE PLANT

For love, and beauty, and delight,
There is no death nor change: their might
Exceeds our organs, which endure
No light, being themselves obscure.

1820.

A VISION OF THE SEA

'TIS the terror of tempest. The rags of the sail
Are flickering in ribbons within the fierce gale:
From the stark night of vapours the dim rain is driven,
And when lightning is loosed, like a deluge from Heaven,
She sees the black trunks of the waterspouts spin
And bend, as if Heaven was ruining in,
Which they seemed to sustain with their terrible mass
As if ocean had sunk from beneath them: they pass
To their graves in the deep with an earthquake of sound,
And the waves and the thunders, made silent around,
Leave the wind to its echo. The vessel, now tossed
Through the low-trailing rack of the tempest, is lost
In the skirts of the thunder-cloud: now down the sweep
Of the wind-cloven wave to the chasm of the deep
It sinks, and the walls of the watery vale
Whose depths of dread calm are unmoved by the gale,
Dim mirrors of ruin, hang gleaming about;
While the surf, like a chaos of stars, like a rout
Of death-flames, like whirlpools of fire-flowing iron,
With splendour and terror the black ship environ,
Or like sulphur-flakes hurled from a mine of pale fire
In fountains spout o'er it. In many a spire
The pyramid-billows with white points of brine
In the cope of the lightning inconstantly shine,

200

A VISION OF THE SEA

As piercing the sky from the floor of the sea.
The great ship seems splitting! it cracks as a tree,
While an earthquake is splintering its root, ere the blast
Of the whirlwind that stripped it of branches has passed.
The intense thunder-balls which are raining from Heaven
Have shattered its mast, and it stands black and riven.
The chinks suck destruction. The heavy dead hulk
On the living sea rolls an inanimate bulk,
Like a corpse on the clay which is hungering to fold
Its corruption around it. Meanwhile, from the hold,
One deck is burst up by the waters below,
And it splits like the ice when the thaw-breezes blow
O'er the lakes of the desert! Who sit on the other?
Is that all the crew that lie burying each other,
Like the dead in a breach, round the foremast? Are those
Twin tigers, who burst, when the waters arose,
In the agony of terror, their chains in the hold;
(What now makes them tame, is what then made them bold;)
Who crouch, side by side, and have driven, like a crank,
The deep grip of their claws through the vibrating plank:—
Are these all? Nine weeks the tall vessel had lain
On the windless expanse of the watery plain,
Where the death-darting sun cast no shadow at noon,
And there seemed to be fire in the beams of the moon,
Till a lead-coloured fog gathered up from the deep,
Whose breath was quick pestilence; then, the cold sleep

A VISION OF THE SEA

Crept, like blight through the ears of a thick field of corn,
O'er the populous vessel. And even and morn,
With their hammocks for coffins the seamen aghast
Like dead men the dead limbs of their comrades cast
Down the deep, which closed on them above and around,
And the sharks and the dogfish their grave-clothes unbound,
And were glutted like Jews with this manna rained down
From God on their wilderness. One after one
The mariners died; on the eve of this day,
When the tempest was gathering in cloudy array,
But seven remained. Six the thunder has smitten,
And they lie black as mummies on which Time has written
His scorn of the embalmer; the seventh, from the deck
An oak-splinter pierced through his breast and his back,
And hung out to the tempest, a wreck on the wreck.
No more? At the helm sits a woman more fair
Than Heaven, when, unbinding its star-braided hair,
It sinks with the sun on the earth and the sea.
She clasps a bright child on her upgathered knee;
It laughs at the lightning, it mocks the mixed thunder
Of the air and the sea, with desire and with wonder
It is beckoning the tigers to rise and come near,
It would play with those eyes where the radiance of fear
Is outshining the meteors; its bosom beats high,
The heart-fire of pleasure has kindled its eye,
While its mother's is lustreless. 'Smile not, my child,

A VISION OF THE SEA

But sleep deeply and sweetly, and so be beguiled
Of the pang that awaits us, whatever that be,
So dreadful since thou must divide it with me!
Dream, sleep! This pale bosom, thy cradle and bed,
Will it rock thee not, infant? 'Tis beating with dread!
Alas! what is life, what is death, what are we,
That when the ship sinks we no longer may be?
What! to see thee no more, and to feel thee no more?
To be after life what we have been before?
Not to touch those sweet hands? Not to look on those eyes,
Those lips, and that hair,—all the smiling disguise
Thou yet wearest, sweet Spirit, which I, day by day,
Have so long called my child, but which now fades away
Like a rainbow, and I the fallen shower?'—Lo! the ship
Is settling, it topples, the leeward ports dip;
The tigers leap up when they feel the slow brine
Crawling inch by inch on them; hair, ears, limbs, and eyne,
Stand rigid with horror; a loud, long, hoarse cry
Bursts at once from their vitals tremendously,
And 'tis borne down the mountainous vale of the wave,
Rebounding, like thunder, from crag to cave,
Mixed with the clash of the lashing rain,
Hurried on by the might of the hurricane:
The hurricane came from the west, and passed on
By the path of the gate of the eastern sun,
Transversely dividing the stream of the storm;

A VISION OF THE SEA

As an arrowy serpent, pursuing the form
Of an elephant, bursts through the brakes of the waste.
Black as a cormorant the screaming blast,
Between Ocean and Heaven, like an ocean, passed,
Till it came to the clouds on the verge of the world
Which, based on the sea and to Heaven upcurled,
Like columns and walls did surround and sustain
The dome of the tempest; it rent them in twain,
As a flood rends its barriers of mountainous crag:
And the dense clouds in many a ruin and rag,
Like the stones of a temple ere earthquake has passed,
Like the dust of its fall, on the whirlwind are cast;
They are scattered like foam on the torrent; and where
The wind has burst out through the chasm, from the air
Of clear morning the beams of the sunrise flow in,
Unimpeded, keen, golden, and crystalline,
Banded armies of light and of air; at one gate
They encounter, but interpenetrate.
And that breach in the tempest is widening away,
And the caverns of cloud are torn up by the day,
And the fierce winds are sinking with weary wings,
Lulled by the motion and murmurings
And the long glassy heave of the rocking sea,
And overhead glorious, but dreadful to see,
The wrecks of the tempest, like vapours of gold,
Are consuming in sunrise. The heaped waves behold

A VISION OF THE SEA

The deep calm of blue Heaven dilating above,
And, like passions made still by the presence of Love,
Beneath the clear surface reflecting it slide
Tremulous with soft influence; extending its tide
From the Andes to Atlas, round mountain and isle,
Round sea-birds and wrecks, paved with Heaven's azure smile,
The wide world of waters is vibrating. Where
Is the ship? On the verge of the wave where it lay
One tiger is mingled in ghastly affray
With a sea-snake. The foam and the smoke of the battle
Stain the clear air with sunbows; the jar, and the rattle
Of solid bones crushed by the infinite stress
Of the snake's adamantine voluminousness;
And the hum of the hot blood that spouts and rains
Where the gripe of the tiger has wounded the veins
Swollen with rage, strength, and effort; the whirl and the splash
As of some hideous engine whose brazen teeth smash
The thin winds and soft waves into thunder; the screams
And hissings crawl fast o'er the smooth ocean-streams,
Each sound like a centipede. Near this commotion,
A blue shark is hanging within the blue ocean,
The fin-wingèd tomb of the victor. The other
Is winning his way from the fate of his brother
To his own with the speed of despair. Lo! a boat
Advances; twelve rowers with the impulse of thought
Urge on the keen keel, —the brine foams. At the stern

A VISION OF THE SEA

Three marksmen stand levelling. Hot bullets burn
In the breast of the tiger, which yet bears him on
To his refuge and ruin. One fragment alone, —
'Tis dwindling and sinking, 'tis now almost gone, —
Of the wreck of the vessel peers out of the sea.
With her left hand she grasps it impetuously,
With her right she sustains her fair infant. Death, Fear,
Love, Beauty, are mixed in the atmosphere,
Which trembles and burns with the fervour of dread
Around her wild eyes, her bright hand, and her head,
Like a meteor of light o'er the waters! her child
Is yet smiling, and playing, and murmuring; so smiled
The false deep ere the storm. Like a sister and brother
The child and the ocean still smile on each other,
Whilst —

1820.

206

ARETHUSA

I

ARETHUSA arose
From her couch of snows
In the Acroceraunian mountains, —
From cloud and from crag,
With many a jag,
Shepherding her bright fountains.
She leapt down the rocks,
With her rainbow locks
Streaming among the streams; —
Her steps paved with green
The downward ravine
Which slopes to the western gleams;
And gliding and springing
She went, ever singing,
In murmurs as soft as sleep;
The Earth seemed to love her,
And Heaven smiled above her,
As she lingered towards the deep.

2

Then Alpheus bold,
On his glacier cold,
With his trident the mountains strook;

ARETHUSA

And opened a chasm
In the rocks—with the spasm
All Erymanthus shook.
And the black south wind
It unsealed behind
The urns of the silent snow,
And earthquake and thunder
Did rend in sunder
The bars of the springs below.
And the beard and the hair
Of the River-god were
Seen through the torrent's sweep,
As he followed the light
Of the fleet nymph's flight
To the brink of the Dorian deep.

3

'Oh, save me! Oh, guide me!
And bid the deep hide me,
For he grasps me now by the hair!'
The loud Ocean heard,
To its blue depth stirred,
And divided at her prayer;
And under the water
The Earth's white daughter
Fled like a sunny beam;

ARETHUSA

Behind her descended
Her billows, unblended
With the brackish Dorian stream:—
　　Like a gloomy stain
　　On the emerald main
Alpheus rushed behind, —
　　As an eagle pursuing
　　A dove to its ruin
Down the streams of the cloudy wind.

4

　　Under the bowers
　　Where the Ocean Powers
Sit on their pearlèd thrones;
　　Through the coral woods
　　Of the weltering floods,
Over heaps of unvalued stones;
　　Through the dim beams
　　Which amid the streams
Weave a network of coloured light;
　　And under the caves,
　　Where the shadowy waves
Are as green as the forest's night:—
　　Outspeeding the shark,
　　And the sword-fish dark,
Under the Ocean's foam,

ARETHUSA

And up through the rifts
Of the mountain clifts
They passed to their Dorian home.

5

And now from their fountains
In Enna's mountains,
Down one vale where the morning basks,
Like friends once parted
Grown single-hearted,
They ply their watery tasks.
At sunrise they leap
From their cradles steep
In the cave of the shelving hill;
At noontide they flow
Through the woods below
And the meadows of asphodel;
And at night they sleep
In the rocking deep
Beneath the Ortygian shore;—
Like spirits that lie
In the azure sky
When they love but live no more.

1820.

LETTER TO MARIA GISBORNE

Leghorn, July 1, 1820

THE spider spreads her webs, whether she be
In poet's tower, cellar, or barn, or tree;
The silk-worm in the dark green mulberry leaves
His winding sheet and cradle ever weaves;
So I, a thing whom moralists call worm,
Sit spinning still round this decaying form,
From the fine threads of rare and subtle thought—
No net of words in garish colours wrought
To catch the idle buzzers of the day—
But a soft cell, where when that fades away,
Memory may clothe in wings my living name
And feed it with the asphodels of fame,
Which in those hearts which must remember me
Grow, making love an immortality.

Whoever should behold me now, I wist,
Would think I were a mighty mechanist,
Bent with sublime Archimedean art
To breathe a soul into the iron heart
Of some machine portentous, or strange gin,
Which by the force of figured spells might win
Its way over the sea, and sport therein;
For round the walls are hung dread engines, such

LETTER TO MARIA GISBORNE

As Vulcan never wrought for Jove to clutch
Ixion or the Titan:—or the quick
Wit of that man of God, St. Dominic,
To convince Atheist, Turk, or Heretic,
Or those in philanthropic council met,
Who thought to pay some interest for the debt
They owed to Jesus Christ for their salvation,
By giving a faint foretaste of damnation
To Shakespeare, Sidney, Spenser, and the rest
Who made our land an island of the blest,
When lamp-like Spain, who now relumes her fire
On Freedom's hearth, grew dim with Empire:—
With thumbscrews, wheels, with tooth and spike and jag,
Which fishers found under the utmost crag
Of Cornwall and the storm-encompassed isles,
Where to the sky the rude sea rarely smiles
Unless in treacherous wrath, as on the morn
When the exulting elements in scorn,
Satiated with destroyed destruction, lay
Sleeping in beauty on their mangled prey,
As panthers sleep;—and other strange and dread
Magical forms the brick floor overspread, —
Proteus transformed to metal did not make
More figures, or more strange; nor did he take
Such shapes of unintelligible brass,
Or heap himself in such a horrid mass

LETTER TO MARIA GISBORNE

Of tin and iron not to be understood;
And forms of unimaginable wood,
To puzzle Tubal Cain and all his brood:
Great screws, and cones, and wheels, and groovèd blocks,
The elements of what will stand the shocks
Of wave and wind and time. —Upon the table
More knacks and quips there be than I am able
To catalogize in this verse of mine:—
A pretty bowl of wood—not full of wine,
But quicksilver; that dew which the gnomes drink
When at their subterranean toil they swink,
Pledging the demons of the earthquake, who
Reply to them in lava—cry halloo!
And call out to the cities o'er their head, —
Roofs, towers, and shrines, the dying and the dead,
Crash through the chinks of earth—and then all quaff
Another rouse, and hold their sides and laugh.
This quicksilver no gnome has drunk—within
The walnut bowl it lies, veinèd and thin,
In colour like the wake of light that stains
The Tuscan deep, when from the moist moon rains
The inmost shower of its white fire—the breeze
Is still—blue Heaven smiles over the pale seas.
And in this bowl of quicksilver—for I
Yield to the impulse of an infancy
Outlasting manhood—I have made to float

LETTER TO MARIA GISBORNE

A rude idealism of a paper boat:—
A hollow screw with cogs—Henry will know
The thing I mean and laugh at me,—if so
He fears not I should do more mischief.—Next
Lie bills and calculations much perplexed,
With steam-boats, frigates, and machinery quaint
Traced over them in blue and yellow paint.
Then comes a range of mathematical
Instruments, for plans nautical and statical;
A heap of rosin, a queer broken glass
With ink in it;—a china cup that was
What it will never be again, I think,—
A thing from which sweet lips were wont to drink
The liquor doctors rail at—and which I
Will quaff in spite of them—and when we die
We'll toss up who died first of drinking tea,
And cry out,—'Heads or tails?' where'er we be.
Near that a dusty paint-box, some odd hooks,
A half-burnt match, an ivory block, three books,
Where conic sections, spherics, logarithms,
To great Laplace, from Saunderson and Sims,
Lie heaped in their harmonious disarray
Of figures,—disentangle them who may.
Baron de Tott's Memoirs beside them lie,
And some odd volumes of old chemistry.
Near those a most inexplicable thing,

LETTER TO MARIA GISBORNE

With lead in the middle—I'm conjecturing
How to make Henry understand; but no—
I'll leave, as Spenser says, with many mo,
This secret in the pregnant womb of time,
Too vast a matter for so weak a rhyme.

And here like some weird Archimage sit I,
Plotting dark spells, and devilish enginery,
The self-impelling steam-wheels of the mind
Which pump up oaths from clergymen, and grind
The gentle spirit of our meek reviews
Into a powdery foam of salt abuse,
Ruffling the ocean of their self-content;—
I sit—and smile or sigh as is my bent,
But not for them—Libeccio rushes round
With an inconstant and an idle sound,
I heed him more than them—the thunder-smoke
Is gathering on the mountains, like a cloak
Folded athwart their shoulders broad and bare;
The ripe corn under the undulating air
Undulates like an ocean;—and the vines
Are trembling wide in all their trellised lines—
The murmur of the awakening sea doth fill
The empty pauses of the blast;—the hill
Looks hoary through the white electric rain,
And from the glens beyond, in sullen strain,

LETTER TO MARIA GISBORNE

The interrupted thunder howls; above
One chasm of Heaven smiles, like the eye of Love
On the unquiet world;—while such things are,
How could one worth your friendship heed the war
Of worms? the shriek of the world's carrion jays,
Their censure, or their wonder, or their praise?

You are not here! the quaint witch Memory sees,
In vacant chairs, your absent images,
And points where once you sat, and now should be
But are not.—I demand if ever we
Shall meet as then we met;—and she replies,
Veiling in awe her second-sighted eyes;
'I know the past alone—but summon home
My sister Hope,—she speaks of all to come.'
But I, an old diviner, who knew well
Every false verse of that sweet oracle,
Turned to the sad enchantress once again,
And sought a respite from my gentle pain,
In citing every passage o'er and o'er
Of our communion—how on the sea-shore
We watched the ocean and the sky together,
Under the roof of blue Italian weather;
How I ran home through last year's thunder-storm,
And felt the transverse lightning linger warm
Upon my cheek—and how we often made

LETTER TO MARIA GISBORNE

Feasts for each other, where good will outweighed
The frugal luxury of our country cheer,
As well it might, were it less firm and clear
Than ours must ever be;—and how we spun
A shroud of talk to hide us from the sun
Of this familiar life, which seems to be
But is not:—or is but quaint mockery
Of all we would believe, and sadly blame
The jarring and inexplicable frame
Of this wrong world:—and then anatomize
The purposes and thoughts of men whose eyes
Were closed in distant years;—or widely guess
The issue of the earth's great business,
When we shall be as we no longer are—
Like babbling gossips safe, who hear the war
Of winds, and sigh, but tremble not;—or how
You listened to some interrupted flow
Of visionary rhyme,—in joy and pain
Struck from the inmost fountains of my brain,
With little skill perhaps;—or how we sought
Those deepest wells of passion or of thought
Wrought by wise poets in the waste of years,
Staining their sacred waters with our tears;
Quenching a thirst ever to be renewed!
Or how I, wisest lady! then endued
The language of a land which now is free,

LETTER TO MARIA GISBORNE

And, winged with thoughts of truth and majesty,
Flits round the tyrant's sceptre like a cloud,
And bursts the peopled prisons, and cries aloud,
'My name is Legion!'—that majestic tongue
Which Calderon over the desert flung
Of ages and of nations; and which found
An echo in our hearts, and with the sound
Startled oblivion;—thou wert then to me
As is a nurse—when inarticulately
A child would talk as its grown parents do.
If living winds the rapid clouds pursue,
If hawks chase doves through the aethereal way,
Huntsmen the innocent deer, and beasts their prey,
Why should not we rouse with the spirit's blast
Out of the forest of the pathless past
These recollected pleasures?
                                        You are now
In London, that great sea, whose ebb and flow
At once is deaf and loud, and on the shore
Vomits its wrecks, and still howls on for more.
Yet in its depth what treasures! You will see
That which was Godwin,—greater none than he
Though fallen—and fallen on evil times—to stand
Among the spirits of our age and land,
Before the dread tribunal of *to come*
The foremost,—while Rebuke cowers pale and dumb.

LETTER TO MARIA GISBORNE

You will see Coleridge—he who sits obscure
In the exceeding lustre and the pure
Intense irradiation of a mind,
Which, with its own internal lightning blind,
Flags wearily through darkness and despair—
A cloud-encircled meteor of the air,
A hooded eagle among blinking owls. —
You will see Hunt—one of those happy souls
Which are the salt of the earth, and without whom
This world would smell like what it is—a tomb;
Who is, what others seem; his room no doubt
Is still adorned with many a cast from Shout,
With graceful flowers tastefully placed about;
And coronals of bay from ribbons hung,
And brighter wreaths in neat disorder flung;
The gifts of the most learned among some dozens
Of female friends, sisters-in-law, and cousins.
And there is he with his eternal puns,
Which beat the dullest brain for smiles, like duns
Thundering for money at a poet's door;
Alas! it is no use to say, 'I'm poor!'
Or oft in graver mood, when he will look
Things wiser than were ever read in book,
Except in Shakespeare's wisest tenderness. —
You will see Hogg,—and I cannot express
His virtues,—though I know that they are great,

LETTER TO MARIA GISBORNE

Because he locks, then barricades the gate
Within which they inhabit;—of his wit
And wisdom, you'll cry out when you are bit.
He is a pearl within an oyster shell,
One of the richest of the deep;—and there
Is English Peacock, with his mountain Fair,
Turned into a Flamingo;—that shy bird
That gleams i' the Indian air—have you not heard
When a man marries, dies, or turns Hindoo,
His best friends hear no more of him?—but you
Will see him, and will like him too, I hope,
With the milk-white Snowdonian Antelope
Matched with this cameleopard—his fine wit
Makes such a wound, the knife is lost in it;
A strain too learnèd for a shallow age,
Too wise for selfish bigots; let his page,
Which charms the chosen spirits of the time,
Fold itself up for the serener clime
Of years to come, and find its recompense
In that just expectation.—Wit and sense,
Virtue and human knowledge; all that might
Make this dull world a business of delight,
Are all combined in Horace Smith.—And these,
With some exceptions, which I need not tease
Your patience by descanting on,—are all
You and I know in London.

LETTER TO MARIA GISBORNE

I recall

My thoughts, and bid you look upon the night.
As water does a sponge, so the moonlight
Fills the void, hollow, universal air—
What see you?—unpavilioned Heaven is fair,
Whether the moon, into her chamber gone,
Leaves midnight to the golden stars, or wan
Climbs with diminished beams the azure steep;
Or whether clouds sail o'er the inverse deep,
Piloted by the many-wandering blast,
And the rare stars rush through them dim and fast:—
All this is beautiful in every land. —
But what see you beside?—a shabby stand
Of Hackney coaches—a brick house or wall
Fencing some lonely court, white with the scrawl
Of our unhappy politics;—or worse—
A wretched woman reeling by, whose curse
Mixed with the watchman's, partner of her trade,
You must accept in place of serenade—
Or yellow-haired Pollonia murmuring
To Henry, some unutterable thing.
I see a chaos of green leaves and fruit
Built round dark caverns, even to the root
Of the living stems that feed them—in whose bowers
There sleep in their dark dew the folded flowers;
Beyond, the surface of the unsickled corn

LETTER TO MARIA GISBORNE

Trembles not in the slumbering air, and borne
In circles quaint, and ever-changing dance,
Like wingèd stars the fire-flies flash and glance,
Pale in the open moonshine, but each one
Under the dark trees seems a little sun,
A meteor tamed; a fixed star gone astray
From the silver regions of the milky way;—
Afar the Contadino's song is heard,
Rude, but made sweet by distance—and a bird
Which cannot be the Nightingale, and yet
I know none else that sings so sweet as it
At this late hour;—and then all is still—
Now—Italy or London, which you will!

Next winter you must pass with me; I'll have
My house by that time turned into a grave
Of dead despondence and low-thoughted care,
And all the dreams which our tormentors are;
Oh! that Hunt, Hogg, Peacock, and Smith were there,
With everything belonging to them fair!—
We will have books, Spanish, Italian, Greek;
And ask one week to make another week
As like his father, as I'm unlike mine,
Which is not his fault, as you may divine.
Though we eat little flesh and drink no wine,
Yet let's be merry: we'll have tea and toast;

LETTER TO MARIA GISBORNE

Custards for supper, and an endless host
Of syllabubs and jellies and mince-pies,
And other such lady-like luxuries, —
Feasting on which we will philosophize!
And we'll have fires out of the Grand Duke's wood,
To thaw the six weeks' winter in our blood.
And then we'll talk;—what shall we talk about?
Oh! there are themes enough for many a bout
Of thought-entangled descant;—as to nerves—
With cones and parallelograms and curves
I've sworn to strangle them if once they dare
To bother me—when you are with me there.
And they shall never more sip laudanum,
From Helicon or Himeros[1];—well, come,
And in despite of God and of the devil,
We'll make our friendly philosophic revel
Outlast the leafless time; till buds and flowers
Warn the obscure inevitable hours,
Sweet meeting by sad parting to renew;—
'To-morrow to fresh woods and pastures new.'

                                        1820.

[1] "Ιμεροc, from which the river Himera was named,
is, with some slight shade of difference, a synonym of
Love.

THE WITCH OF ATLAS

*

TO MARY

On her objecting to the following poem, upon the
score of its containing no human interest

I

HOW, my dear Mary, —are you critic-bitten
   (For vipers kill, though dead) by some review,
That you condemn these verses I have written,
   Because they tell no story, false or true?
What, though no mice are caught by a young kitten,
   May it not leap and play as grown cats do,
Till its claws come? Prithee, for this one time,
Content thee with a visionary rhyme.

2

What hand would crush the silken-wingèd fly,
   The youngest of inconstant April's minions,
Because it cannot climb the purest sky,
   Where the swan sings, amid the sun's dominions?
Not thine. Thou knowest 'tis its doom to die,
   When Day shall hide within her twilight pinions
The lucent eyes, and the eternal smile,
Serene as thine, which lent it life awhile.

224

THE WITCH OF ATLAS

3

To thy fair feet a wingèd Vision came,
    Whose date should have been longer than a day,
And o'er thy head did beat its wings for fame,
    And in thy sight its fading plumes display;
The watery bow burned in the evening flame,
    But the shower fell, the swift Sun went his way —
And that is dead. — O, let me not believe
That anything of mine is fit to live!

4

Wordsworth informs us he was nineteen years
    Considering and retouching Peter Bell;
Watering his laurels with the killing tears
    Of slow, dull care, so that their roots to Hell
Might pierce, and their wide branches blot the spheres
    Of Heaven, with dewy leaves and flowers; this well
May be, for Heaven and Earth conspire to foil
The over-busy gardener's blundering toil.

5

My Witch indeed is not so sweet a creature
    As Ruth or Lucy, whom his graceful praise
Clothes for our grandsons — but she matches Peter,
    Though he took nineteen years, and she three days
In dressing. Light the vest of flowing metre
    She wears; he, proud as dandy with his stays,

THE WITCH OF ATLAS

Has hung upon his wiry limbs a dress
Like King Lear's 'looped and windowed raggedness.'

6

If you strip Peter, you will see a fellow
   Scorched by Hell's hyperequatorial climate
Into a kind of a sulphureous yellow:
   A lean mark, hardly fit to fling a rhyme at;
In shape a Scaramouch, in hue Othello.
   If you unveil my Witch, no priest nor primate
Can shrive you of that sin, —if sin there be
In love, when it becomes idolatry.

THE WITCH OF ATLAS

1

B EFORE those cruel Twins, whom at one birth
 Incestuous Change bore to her father Time,
Error and Truth, had hunted from the Earth
   All those bright natures which adorned its prime,
And left us nothing to believe in, worth
   The pains of putting into learnèd rhyme,
A lady-witch there lived on Atlas' mountain
Within a cavern, by a secret fountain.

2

Her mother was one of the Atlantides:
   The all-beholding Sun had ne'er beholden
In his wide voyage o'er continents and seas
   So fair a creature, as she lay enfolden
In the warm shadow of her loveliness;—
   He kissed her with his beams, and made all golden
The chamber of gray rock in which she lay—
She, in that dream of joy, dissolved away.

3

'Tis said, she first was changed into a vapour,
   And then into a cloud, such clouds as flit,
Like splendour-wingèd moths about a taper,

THE WITCH OF ATLAS

Round the red west when the sun dies in it:
And then into a meteor, such as caper
   On hill-tops when the moon is in a fit:
Then, into one of those mysterious stars
Which hide themselves between the Earth and Mars.

4

Ten times the Mother of the Months had bent
   Her bow beside the folding-star, and bidden
With that bright sign the billows to indent
   The sea-deserted sand—like children chidden,
At her command they ever came and went—
   Since in that cave a dewy splendour hidden
Took shape and motion: with the living form
Of this embodied Power, the cave grew warm.

5

A lovely lady garmented in light
   From her own beauty—deep her eyes, as are
Two openings of unfathomable night
   Seen through a Temple's cloven roof—her hair
Dark—the dim brain whirls dizzy with delight,
   Picturing her form; her soft smiles shone afar,
And her low voice was heard like love, and drew
All living things towards this wonder new.

228

THE WITCH OF ATLAS

6

And first the spotted cameleopard came,
    And then the wise and fearless elephant;
Then the sly serpent, in the golden flame
    Of his own volumes intervolved;—all gaunt
And sanguine beasts her gentle looks made tame.
    They drank before her at her sacred fount;
And every beast of beating heart grew bold,
Such gentleness and power even to behold.

7

The brinded lioness led forth her young,
    That she might teach them how they should forego
Their inborn thirst of death; the pard unstrung
    His sinews at her feet, and sought to know
With looks whose motions spoke without a tongue
    How he might be as gentle as the doe.
The magic circle of her voice and eyes
All savage natures did imparadise.

8

And old Silenus, shaking a green stick
    Of lilies, and the wood-gods in a crew
Came, blithe, as in the olive copses thick
    Cicadae are, drunk with the noonday dew:
And Dryope and Faunus followed quick,
    Teasing the God to sing them something new;

THE WITCH OF ATLAS

Till in this cave they found the lady lone,
Sitting upon a seat of emerald stone.

9

And universal Pan, 'tis said, was there,
    And though none saw him, — through the adamant
Of the deep mountains, through the trackless air,
    And through those living spirits, like a want,
He passed out of his everlasting lair
    Where the quick heart of the great world doth pant,
And felt that wondrous lady all alone, —
And she felt him, upon her emerald throne.

10

And every nymph of stream and spreading tree,
    And every shepherdess of Ocean's flocks,
Who drives her white waves over the green sea,
    And Ocean with the brine on his gray locks,
And quaint Priapus with his company,
    All came, much wondering how the enwombèd rocks
Could have brought forth so beautiful a birth; —
Her love subdued their wonder and their mirth.

11

The herdsmen and the mountain maidens came,
    And the rude kings of pastoral Garamant—
Their spirits shook within them, as a flame
    Stirred by the air under a cavern gaunt:

230

THE WITCH OF ATLAS

Pigmies, and Polyphemes, by many a name,
　　Centaurs, and Satyrs, and such shapes as haunt
Wet clefts, —and lumps neither alive nor dead,
Dog-headed, bosom-eyed, and bird-footed.

12

For she was beautiful—her beauty made
　　The bright world dim, and everything beside
Seemed like the fleeting image of a shade:
　　No thought of living spirit could abide,
Which to her looks had ever been betrayed,
　　On any object in the world so wide,
On any hope within the circling skies,
But on her form, and in her inmost eyes.

13

Which when the lady knew, she took her spindle
　　And twined three threads of fleecy mist, and three
Long lines of light, such as the dawn may kindle
　　The clouds and waves and mountains with; and she
As many star-beams, ere their lamps could dwindle
　　In the belated moon, wound skilfully;
And with these threads a subtle veil she wove—
A shadow for the splendour of her love.

14

The deep recesses of her odorous dwelling
　　Were stored with magic treasures—sounds of air,

THE WITCH OF ATLAS

Which had the power all spirits of compelling,
 Folded in cells of crystal silence there;
Such as we hear in youth, and think the feeling
 Will never die—yet ere we are aware,
The feeling and the sound are fled and gone,
And the regret they leave remains alone.

15

And there lay Visions swift, and sweet, and quaint,
 Each in its thin sheath, like a chrysalis,
Some eager to burst forth, some weak and faint
 With the soft burthen of intensest bliss.
It was its work to bear to many a saint
 Whose heart adores the shrine which holiest is,
Even Love's:—and others white, green, gray, and black,
And of all shapes—and each was at her beck.

16

And odours in a kind of aviary
 Of ever-blooming Eden-trees she kept,
Clipped in a floating net, a love-sick Fairy
 Had woven from dew-beams while the moon yet slept;
As bats at the wired window of a dairy,
 They beat their vans; and each was an adept,
When loosed and missioned, making wings of winds,
To stir sweet thoughts or sad, in destined minds.

THE WITCH OF ATLAS

17

And liquors clear and sweet, whose healthful might
   Could medicine the sick soul to happy sleep,
And change eternal death into a night
   Of glorious dreams—or if eyes needs must weep,
Could make their tears all wonder and delight,
   She in her crystal vials did closely keep:
If men could drink of those clear vials, 'tis said
The living were not envied of the dead.

18

Her cave was stored with scrolls of strange device,
   The works of some Saturnian Archimage,
Which taught the expiations at whose price
   Men from the Gods might win that happy age
Too lightly lost, redeeming native vice;
   And which might quench the Earth-consuming rage
Of gold and blood—till men should live and move
Harmonious as the sacred stars above;

19

And how all things that seem untameable,
   Not to be checked and not to be confined,
Obey the spells of Wisdom's wizard skill;
   Time, earth, and fire—the ocean and the wind,
And all their shapes—and man's imperial will;
   And other scrolls whose writings did unbind

THE WITCH OF ATLAS

The inmost lore of Love—let the profane
Tremble to ask what secrets they contain.

20

And wondrous works of substances unknown,
    To which the enchantment of her father's power
Had changed those ragged blocks of savage stone,
    Were heaped in the recesses of her bower;
Carved lamps and chalices, and vials which shone
    In their own golden beams—each like a flower,
Out of whose depth a fire-fly shakes his light
Under a cypress in a starless night.

21

At first she lived alone in this wild home,
    And her own thoughts were each a minister,
Clothing themselves, or with the ocean foam,
    Or with the wind, or with the speed of fire,
To work whatever purposes might come
    Into her mind; such power her mighty Sire
Had girt them with, whether to fly or run,
Through all the regions which he shines upon.

22

The Ocean-nymphs and Hamadryades,
    Oreads and Naiads, with long weedy locks,
Offered to do her bidding through the seas,
    Under the earth, and in the hollow rocks,

THE WITCH OF ATLAS

And far beneath the matted roots of trees,
  And in the gnarlèd heart of stubborn oaks,
So they might live for ever in the light
Of her sweet presence—each a satellite.

23

'This may not be,' the wizard maid replied;
  'The fountains where the Naiades bedew
Their shining hair, at length are drained and dried;
  The solid oaks forget their strength, and strew
Their latest leaf upon the mountains wide;
  The boundless ocean like a drop of dew
Will be consumed—the stubborn centre must
Be scattered, like a cloud of summer dust.

24

'And ye with them will perish, one by one;—
  If I must sigh to think that this shall be,
If I must weep when the surviving Sun
  Shall smile on your decay—oh, ask not me
To love you till your little race is run;
  I cannot die as ye must—over me
Your leaves shall glance—the streams in which ye dwell
Shall be my paths henceforth, and so—farewell!'—

25

She spoke and wept:—the dark and azure well
  Sparkled beneath the shower of her bright tears,

THE WITCH OF ATLAS

And every little circlet where they fell
    Flung to the cavern-roof inconstant spheres
And intertangled lines of light:—a knell
    Of sobbing voices came upon her ears
From those departing Forms, o'er the serene
Of the white streams and of the forest green.

26

All day the wizard lady sate aloof,
    Spelling out scrolls of dread antiquity,
Under the cavern's fountain-lighted roof;
    Or broidering the pictured poesy
Of some high tale upon her growing woof,
    Which the sweet splendour of her smiles could dye
In hues outshining heaven—and ever she
Added some grace to the wrought poesy.

27

While on her hearth lay blazing many a piece
    Of sandal wood, rare gums, and cinnamon;
Men scarcely know how beautiful fire is—
    Each flame of it is as a precious stone
Dissolved in ever-moving light, and this
    Belongs to each and all who gaze upon.
The Witch beheld it not, for in her hand
She held a woof that dimmed the burning brand.

THE WITCH OF ATLAS

28

This lady never slept, but lay in trance
   All night within the fountain—as in sleep.
Its emerald crags glowed in her beauty's glance;
   Through the green splendour of the water deep
She saw the constellations reel and dance
   Like fire-flies—and withal did ever keep
The tenour of her contemplations calm,
With open eyes, closed feet, and folded palm.

29

And when the whirlwinds and the clouds descended
   From the white pinnacles of that cold hill,
She passed at dewfall to a space extended,
   Where in a lawn of flowering asphodel
Amid a wood of pines and cedars blended,
   There yawned an inextinguishable well
Of crimson fire—full even to the brim,
And overflowing all the margin trim.

30

Within the which she lay when the fierce war
   Of wintry winds shook that innocuous liquor
In many a mimic moon and bearded star
   O'er woods and lawns;—the serpent heard it flicker
In sleep, and dreaming still, he crept afar—
   And when the windless snow descended thicker

THE WITCH OF ATLAS

Than autumn leaves, she watched it as it came
Melt on the surface of the level flame.

31

She had a boat, which some say Vulcan wrought
    For Venus, as the chariot of her star;
But it was found too feeble to be fraught
    With all the ardours in that sphere which are,
And so she sold it, and Apollo bought
    And gave it to this daughter: from a car
Changed to the fairest and the lightest boat
Which ever upon mortal stream did float.

32

And others say, that, when but three hours old,
    The first-born Love out of his cradle lept,
And clove dun Chaos with his wings of gold,
    And like a horticultural adept,
Stole a strange seed, and wrapped it up in mould,
    And sowed it in his mother's star, and kept
Watering it all the summer with sweet dew,
And with his wings fanning it as it grew.

33

The plant grew strong and green, the snowy flower
    Fell, and the long and gourd-like fruit began
To turn the light and dew by inward power
    To its own substance; woven tracery ran

THE WITCH OF ATLAS

Of light firm texture, ribbed and branching, o'er
   The solid rind, like a leaf's veinèd fan—
Of which Love scooped this boat—and with soft motion
Piloted it round the circumfluous ocean.

34

This boat she moored upon her fount, and lit
   A living spirit within all its frame,
Breathing the soul of swiftness into it.
   Couched on the fountain like a panther tame,
One of the twain at Evan's feet that sit—
   Or as on Vesta's sceptre a swift flame—
Or on blind Homer's heart a wingèd thought,—
In joyous expectation lay the boat.

35

Then by strange art she kneaded fire and snow
   Together, tempering the repugnant mass
With liquid love—all things together grow
   Through which the harmony of love can pass;
And a fair Shape out of her hands did flow—
   A living Image, which did far surpass
In beauty that bright shape of vital stone
Which drew the heart out of Pygmalion.

36

A sexless thing it was, and in its growth
   It seemed to have developed no defect

239

THE WITCH OF ATLAS

Of either sex, yet all the grace of both, —
    In gentleness and strength its limbs were decked;
The bosom swelled lightly with its full youth,
    The countenance was such as might select
Some artist that his skill should never die,
Imaging forth such perfect purity.

37

From its smooth shoulders hung two rapid wings,
    Fit to have borne it to the seventh sphere,
Tipped with the speed of liquid lightenings,
    Dyed in the ardours of the atmosphere:
She led her creature to the boiling springs
    Where the light boat was moored, and said: 'Sit here!'
And pointed to the prow, and took her seat
Beside the rudder, with opposing feet.

38

And down the streams which clove those mountains vast,
    Around their inland islets, and amid
The panther-peopled forests, whose shade cast
    Darkness and odours, and a pleasure hid
In melancholy gloom, the pinnace passed;
    By many a star-surrounded pyramid
Of icy crag cleaving the purple sky,
And caverns yawning round unfathomably.

THE WITCH OF ATLAS

39

The silver noon into that winding dell,
  With slanted gleam athwart the forest tops,
Tempered like golden evening, feebly fell;
  A green and glowing light, like that which drops
From folded lilies in which glow-worms dwell,
  When Earth over her face Night's mantle wraps;
Between the severed mountains lay on high,
Over the stream, a narrow rift of sky.

40

And ever as she went, the Image lay
  With folded wings and unawakened eyes;
And o'er its gentle countenance did play
  The busy dreams, as thick as summer flies,
Chasing the rapid smiles that would not stay,
  And drinking the warm tears, and the sweet sighs
Inhaling, which, with busy murmur vain,
They had aroused from that full heart and brain.

41

And ever down the prone vale, like a cloud
  Upon a stream of wind, the pinnace went:
Now lingering on the pools, in which abode
  The calm and darkness of the deep content
In which they paused; now o'er the shallow road

THE WITCH OF ATLAS

Of white and dancing waters, all besprent
With sand and polished pebbles:—mortal boat
In such a shallow rapid could not float.

42

And down the earthquaking cataracts which shiver
    Their snow-like waters into golden air,
Or under chasms unfathomable ever
    Sepulchre them, till in their rage they tear
A subterranean portal for the river,
    It fled—the circling sunbows did upbear
Its fall down the hoar precipice of spray,
Lighting it far upon its lampless way.

43

And when the wizard lady would ascend
    The labyrinths of some many-winding vale,
Which to the inmost mountain upward tend—
    She called 'Hermaphroditus!'—and the pale
And heavy hue which slumber could extend
    Over its lips and eyes, as on the gale
A rapid shadow from a slope of grass,
Into the darkness of the stream did pass.

44

And it unfurled its heaven-coloured pinions,
    With stars of fire spotting the stream below;
And from above into the Sun's dominions

THE WITCH OF ATLAS

Flinging a glory, like the golden glow
In which Spring clothes her emerald-wingèd minions,
All interwoven with fine feathery snow
And moonlight splendour of intensest rime,
With which frost paints the pines in winter time.

45

And then it winnowed the Elysian air
Which ever hung about that lady bright,
With its aethereal vans—and speeding there,
Like a star up the torrent of the night,
Or a swift eagle in the morning glare
Breasting the whirlwind with impetuous flight,
The pinnace, oared by those enchanted wings,
Clove the fierce streams towards their upper springs.

46

The water flashed, like sunlight by the prow
Of a noon-wandering meteor flung to Heaven;
The still air seemed as if its waves did flow
In tempest down the mountains; loosely driven
The lady's radiant hair streamed to and fro:
Beneath, the billows having vainly striven
Indignant and impetuous, roared to feel
The swift and steady motion of the keel.

THE WITCH OF ATLAS

47

Or, when the weary moon was in the wane,
   Or in the noon of interlunar night,
The lady-witch in visions could not chain
   Her spirit; but sailed forth under the light
Of shooting stars, and bade extend amain
   Its storm-outspeeding wings, the Hermaphrodite;
She to the Austral waters took her way,
Beyond the fabulous Thamondocana, —

48

Where, like a meadow which no scythe has shaven,
   Which rain could never bend, or whirl-blast shake,
With the Antarctic constellations paven,
   Canopus and his crew, lay the Austral lake—
There she would build herself a windless haven
   Out of the clouds whose moving turrets make
The bastions of the storm, when through the sky
The spirits of the tempest thundered by:

49

A haven beneath whose translucent floor
   The tremulous stars sparkled unfathomably,
And around which the solid vapours hoar,
   Based on the level waters, to the sky
Lifted their dreadful crags, and like a shore
   Of wintry mountains, inaccessibly

THE WITCH OF ATLAS

Hemmed in with rifts and precipices gray,
And hanging crags, many a cove and bay.

50

And whilst the outer lake beneath the lash
  Of the wind's scourge, foamed like a wounded thing,
And the incessant hail with stony clash
  Ploughed up the waters, and the flagging wing
Of the roused cormorant in the lightning flash
  Looked like the wreck of some wind-wandering
Fragment of inky thunder-smoke—this haven
Was as a gem to copy Heaven engraven,—

51

On which that lady played her many pranks,
  Circling the image of a shooting star,
Even as a tiger on Hydaspes' banks
  Outspeeds the antelopes which speediest are,
In her light boat; and many quips and cranks
  She played upon the water, till the car
Of the late moon, like a sick matron wan,
To journey from the misty east began.

52

And then she called out of the hollow turrets
  Of those high clouds, white, golden and vermilion,
The armies of her ministering spirits—
  In mighty legions, million after million,

245

THE WITCH OF ATLAS

They came, each troop emblazoning its merits
  On meteor flags; and many a proud pavilion
Of the intertexture of the atmosphere
They pitched upon the plain of the calm mere.

53

They framed the imperial tent of their great Queen
  Of woven exhalations, underlaid
With lambent lightning-fire, as may be seen
  A dome of thin and open ivory inlaid
With crimson silk—cressets from the serene
  Hung there, and on the water for her tread
A tapestry of fleece-like mist was strewn,
Dyed in the beams of the ascending moon.

54

And on a throne o'erlaid with starlight, caught
  Upon those wandering isles of aëry dew,
Which highest shoals of mountain shipwreck not,
  She sate, and heard all that had happened new
Between the earth and moon, since they had brought
  The last intelligence—and now she grew
Pale as that moon, lost in the watery night—
And now she wept, and now she laughed outright.

55

These were tame pleasures; she would often climb
  The steepest ladder of the crudded rack

THE WITCH OF ATLAS

Up to some beakèd cape of cloud sublime,
　　And like Arion on the dolphin's back
Ride singing through the shoreless air; —oft-time
　　Following the serpent lightning's winding track,
She ran upon the platforms of the wind,
And laughed to hear the fire-balls roar behind.

56

And sometimes to those streams of upper air
　　Which whirl the earth in its diurnal round,
She would ascend, and win the spirits there
　　To let her join their chorus. Mortals found
That on those days the sky was calm and fair,
　　And mystic snatches of harmonious sound
Wandered upon the earth where'er she passed,
And happy thoughts of hope, too sweet to last.

57

But her choice sport was, in the hours of sleep,
　　To glide adown old Nilus, where he threads
Egypt and Aethiopia, from the steep
　　Of utmost Axumè, until he spreads,
Like a calm flock of silver-fleecèd sheep,
　　His waters on the plain: and crested heads
Of cities and proud temples gleam amid,
And many a vapour-belted pyramid.

THE WITCH OF ATLAS

58

By Moeris and the Mareotid lakes,
   Strewn with faint blooms like bridal chamber floors,
Where naked boys bridling tame water-snakes,
   Or charioteering ghastly alligators,
Had left on the sweet waters mighty wakes
   Of those huge forms—within the brazen doors
Of the great Labyrinth slept both boy and beast,
Tired with the pomp of their Osirian feast.

59

And where within the surface of the river
   The shadows of the massy temples lie,
And never are erased—but tremble ever
   Like things which every cloud can doom to die,
Through lotus-paven canals, and wheresoever
   The works of man pierced that serenest sky
With tombs, and towers, and fanes, 'twas her delight
To wander in the shadow of the night.

60

With motion like the spirit of that wind
   Whose soft step deepens slumber, her light feet
Passed through the peopled haunts of humankind,
   Scattering sweet visions from her presence sweet,
Through fane, and palace-court, and labyrinth mined
   With many a dark and subterranean street

248

THE WITCH OF ATLAS

Under the Nile, through chambers high and deep
She passed, observing mortals in their sleep.

61

A pleasure sweet doubtless it was to see
   Mortals subdued in all the shapes of sleep.
Here lay two sister twins in infancy;
   There, a lone youth who in his dreams did weep;
Within, two lovers linkèd innocently
   In their loose locks which over both did creep
Like ivy from one stem;—and there lay calm
Old age with snow-bright hair and folded palm.

62

But other troubled forms of sleep she saw,
   Not to be mirrored in a holy song—
Distortions foul of supernatural awe,
   And pale imaginings of visioned wrong;
And all the code of Custom's lawless law
   Written upon the brows of old and young:
'This,' said the wizard maiden, 'is the strife
Which stirs the liquid surface of man's life.'

63

And little did the sight disturb her soul.—
   We, the weak mariners of that wide lake
Where'er its shores extend or billows roll,
   Our course unpiloted and starless make

THE WITCH OF ATLAS

O'er its wild surface to an unknown goal:—
    But she in the calm depths her way could take,
Where in bright bowers immortal forms abide
Beneath the weltering of the restless tide.

64

And she saw princes couched under the glow
    Of sunlike gems; and round each temple-court
In dormitories ranged, row after row,
    She saw the priests asleep—all of one sort—
For all were educated to be so. —
    The peasants in their huts, and in the port
The sailors she saw cradled on the waves,
And the dead lulled within their dreamless graves.

65

And all the forms in which those spirits lay
    Were to her sight like the diaphanous
Veils, in which those sweet ladies oft array
    Their delicate limbs, who would conceal from us
Only their scorn of all concealment: they
    Move in the light of their own beauty thus.
But these and all now lay with sleep upon them,
And little thought a Witch was looking on them.

66

She, all those human figures breathing there,
    Beheld as living spirits—to her eyes

THE WITCH OF ATLAS

The naked beauty of the soul lay bare,
    And often through a rude and worn disguise
She saw the inner form most bright and fair—
    And then she had a charm of strange device,
Which, murmured on mute lips with tender tone,
Could make that spirit mingle with her own.

67

Alas! Aurora, what wouldst thou have given
    For such a charm when Tithon became gray?
Or how much, Venus, of thy silver heaven
    Wouldst thou have yielded, ere Proserpina
Had half (oh! why not all?) the debt forgiven
    Which dear Adonis had been doomed to pay,
To any witch who would have taught you it?
The Heliad doth not know its value yet.

68

'Tis said in after times her spirit free
    Knew what love was, and felt itself alone—
But holy Dian could not chaster be
    Before she stooped to kiss Endymion,
Than now this lady—like a sexless bee
    Tasting all blossoms, and confined to none,
Among those mortal forms, the wizard-maiden
Passed with an eye serene and heart unladen.

THE WITCH OF ATLAS

69

To those she saw most beautiful, she gave
  Strange panacea in a crystal bowl:—
They drank in their deep sleep of that sweet wave,
  And lived thenceforward as if some control,
Mightier than life, were in them; and the grave
  Of such, when death oppressed the weary soul,
Was as a green and overarching bower
Lit by the gems of many a starry flower.

70

For on the night when they were buried, she
  Restored the embalmers' ruining, and shook
The light out of the funeral lamps, to be
  A mimic day within that deathy nook;
And she unwound the woven imagery
  Of second childhood's swaddling bands, and took
The coffin, its last cradle, from its niche,
And threw it with contempt into a ditch.

71

And there the body lay, age after age,
  Mute, breathing, beating, warm, and undecaying,
Like one asleep in a green hermitage,
  With gentle smiles about its eyelids playing,
And living in its dreams beyond the rage
  Of death or life; while they were still arraying

THE WITCH OF ATLAS

In liveries ever new, the rapid, blind
And fleeting generations of mankind.

72

And she would write strange dreams upon the brain
  Of those who were less beautiful, and make
All harsh and crooked purposes more vain
  Than in the desert is the serpent's wake
Which the sand covers—all his evil gain
  The miser in such dreams would rise and shake
Into a beggar's lap;—the lying scribe
Would his own lies betray without a bribe.

73

The priests would write an explanation full,
  Translating hieroglyphics into Greek,
How the God Apis really was a bull,
  And nothing more; and bid the herald stick
The same against the temple doors, and pull
  The old cant down; they licensed all to speak
Whate'er they thought of hawks, and cats, and geese,
By pastoral letters to each diocese.

74

The king would dress an ape up in his crown
  And robes, and seat him on his glorious seat,
And on the right hand of the sunlike throne
  Would place a gaudy mock-bird to repeat

THE WITCH OF ATLAS

The chatterings of the monkey.—Every one
   Of the prone courtiers crawled to kiss the feet
Of their great Emperor, when the morning came,
And kissed—alas, how many kiss the same!

75

The soldiers dreamed that they were blacksmiths, and
   Walked out of quarters in somnambulism;
Round the red anvils you might see them stand
   Like Cyclopses in Vulcan's sooty abysm,
Beating their swords to ploughshares;—in a band
   The gaolers sent those of the liberal schism
Free through the streets of Memphis, much, I wis,
To the annoyance of king Amasis.

76

And timid lovers who had been so coy,
   They hardly knew whether they loved or not,
Would rise out of their rest, and take sweet joy,
   To the fulfilment of their inmost thought;
And when next day the maiden and the boy
   Met one another, both, like sinners caught,
Blushed at the thing which each believed was done
Only in fancy—till the tenth moon shone;

77

And then the Witch would let them take no ill:
   Of many thousand schemes which lovers find,

254

THE WITCH OF ATLAS

The Witch found one,—and so they took their fill
    Of happiness in marriage warm and kind.
Friends who, by practice of some envious skill,
    Were torn apart—a wide wound, mind from mind!—
She did unite again with visions clear
Of deep affection and of truth sincere.

78

These were the pranks she played among the cities
    Of mortal men, and what she did to Sprites
And Gods, entangling them in her sweet ditties
    To do her will, and show their subtle sleights,
I will declare another time; for it is
    A tale more fit for the weird winter nights
Than for these garish summer days, when we
Scarcely believe much more than we can see.

1820.

ORPHEUS

A. Not far from hence. From yonder pointed hill,
Crowned with a ring of oaks, you may behold
A dark and barren field, through which there flows,
Sluggish and black, a deep but narrow stream,
Which the wind ripples not, and the fair moon
Gazes in vain, and finds no mirror there.
Follow the herbless banks of that strange brook
Until you pause beside a darksome pond,
The fountain of this rivulet, whose gush
Cannot be seen, hid by a rayless night
That lives beneath the overhanging rock
That shades the pool—an endless spring of gloom,
Upon whose edge hovers the tender light,
Trembling to mingle with its paramour,—
But, as Syrinx fled Pan, so night flies day,
Or, with most sullen and regardless hate,
Refuses stern her heaven-born embrace.
On one side of this jagged and shapeless hill
There is a cave, from which there eddies up
A pale mist, like aëreal gossamer,
Whose breath destroys all life—awhile it veils
The rock—then, scattered by the wind, it flies
Along the stream, or lingers on the clefts,
Killing the sleepy worms, if aught bide there.

ORPHEUS

Upon the beetling edge of that dark rock
There stands a group of cypresses; not such
As, with a graceful spire and stirring life,
Pierce the pure heaven of your native vale,
Whose branches the air plays among, but not
Disturbs, fearing to spoil their solemn grace;
But blasted and all wearily they stand,
One to another clinging; their weak boughs
Sigh as the wind buffets them, and they shake
Beneath its blasts—a weatherbeaten crew!

    Chorus. What wondrous sound is that, mournful and faint,
But more melodious than the murmuring wind
Which through the columns of a temple glides?

    A. It is the wandering voice of Orpheus' lyre,
Borne by the winds, who sigh that their rude king
Hurries them fast from these air-feeding notes;
But in their speed they bear along with them
The waning sound, scattering it like dew
Upon the startled sense.

    Chorus.   Does he still sing?
Methought he rashly cast away his harp
When he had lost Eurydice.

    A.   Ah, no!
Awhile he paused. As a poor hunted stag
A moment shudders on the fearful brink
Of a swift stream—the cruel hounds press on

ORPHEUS

With deafening yell, the arrows glance and wound, —
He plunges in: so Orpheus, seized and torn
By the sharp fangs of an insatiate grief,
Maenad-like waved his lyre in the bright air,
And wildly shrieked 'Where she is, it is dark!'
And then he struck from forth the strings a sound
Of deep and fearful melody. Alas!
In times long past, when fair Eurydice
With her bright eyes sat listening by his side,
He gently sang of high and heavenly themes.
As in a brook, fretted with little waves
By the light airs of spring—each riplet makes
A many-sided mirror for the sun,
While it flows musically through green banks,
Ceaseless and pauseless, ever clear and fresh,
So flowed his song, reflecting the deep joy
And tender love that fed those sweetest notes,
The heavenly offspring of ambrosial food.
But that is past. Returning from drear Hell,
He chose a lonely seat of unhewn stone,
Blackened with lichens, on a herbless plain.
Then from the deep and overflowing spring
Of his eternal ever-moving grief
There rose to Heaven a sound of angry song.
'Tis as a mighty cataract that parts
Two sister rocks with waters swift and strong,

ORPHEUS

And casts itself with horrid roar and din
Adown a steep; from a perennial source
It ever flows and falls, and breaks the air
With loud and fierce, but most harmonious roar,
And as it falls casts up a vaporous spray
Which the sun clothes in hues of Iris light.
Thus the tempestuous torrent of his grief
Is clothed in sweetest sounds and varying words
Of poesy. Unlike all human works,
It never slackens, and through every change
Wisdom and beauty and the power divine
Of mighty poesy together dwell,
Mingling in sweet accord. As I have seen
A fierce south blast tear through the darkened sky,
Driving along a rack of wingèd clouds,
Which may not pause, but ever hurry on,
As their wild shepherd wills them, while the stars,
Twinkling and dim, peep from between the plumes.
Anon the sky is cleared, and the high dome
Of serene Heaven, starred with fiery flowers,
Shuts in the shaken earth; or the still moon
Swiftly, yet gracefully, begins her walk,
Rising all bright behind the eastern hills.
I talk of moon, and wind, and stars, and not
Of song; but, would I echo his high song,
Nature must lend me words ne'er used before,

ORPHEUS

Or I must borrow from her perfect works,
To picture forth his perfect attributes.
He does no longer sit upon his throne
Of rock upon a desert herbless plain,
For the evergreen and knotted ilexes,
And cypresses that seldom wave their boughs,
And sea-green olives with their grateful fruit,
And elms dragging along the twisted vines,
Which drop their berries as they follow fast,
And blackthorn bushes with their infant race
Of blushing rose-blooms; beeches, to lovers dear
And weeping willow trees; all swift or slow,
As their huge boughs or lighter dress permit,
Have circled in his throne, and Earth herself
Has sent from her maternal breast a growth
Of starlike flowers and herbs of odour sweet,
To pave the temple that his poesy
Has framed, while near his feet grim lions couch,
And kids, fearless from love, creep near his lair.
Even the blind worms seem to feel the sound.
The birds are silent, hanging down their heads,
Perched on the lowest branches of the trees;
Not even the nightingale intrudes a note
In rivalry, but all entranced she listens.

1820.

FIORDISPINA

THE season was the childhood of sweet June,
    Whose sunny hours from morning until noon
Went creeping through the day with silent feet,
Each with its load of pleasure; slow yet sweet;
Like the long years of blest Eternity
Never to be developed. Joy to thee,
Fiordispina and thy Cosimo,
For thou the wonders of the depth canst know
Of this unfathomable flood of hours,
Sparkling beneath the heaven which embowers—

   .   .   .   .   .

They were two cousins, almost like to twins,
Except that from the catalogue of sins
Nature had rased their love—which could not be
But by dissevering their nativity.
And so they grew together like two flowers
Upon one stem, which the same beams and showers
Lull or awaken in their purple prime,
Which the same hand will gather—the same clime
Shake with decay. This fair day smiles to see
All those who love—and who e'er loved like thee,
Fiordispina? Scarcely Cosimo,
Within whose bosom and whose brain now glow
The ardours of a vision which obscure

FIORDISPINA

The very idol of its portraiture.
He faints, dissolved into a sea of love;
But thou art as a planet sphered above;
But thou art Love itself—ruling the motion
Of his subjected spirit: such emotion
Must end in sin and sorrow, if sweet May
Had not brought forth this morn—your wedding-day.

    .   .   .   .   .

'Lie there; sleep awhile in your own dew,
Ye faint-eyed children of the   Hours,'
Fiordispina said, and threw the flowers
Which she had from the breathing—

    .   .   .   .   .

A table near of polished porphyry.
They seemed to wear a beauty from the eye
That looked on them—a fragrance from the touch
Whose warmth   checked their life; a light such
As sleepers wear, lulled by the voice they love,
                        which did reprove
The childish pity that she felt for them,
And a   remorse that from their stem
She had divided such fair shapes   made
A feeling in the   which was a shade
Of gentle beauty on the flowers: there lay
All gems that make the earth's dark bosom gay.
        rods of myrtle-buds and lemon-blooms,

FIORDISPINA

And that leaf tinted lightly which assumes
The livery of unremembered snow—
Violets whose eyes have drunk—

   .   .   .   .   .

Fiordispina and her nurse are now
Upon the steps of the high portico;
Under the withered arm of Media
She flings her glowing arm

   .   .   .   .   .

        step by step and stair by stair,
That withered woman, gray and white and brown—
More like a trunk by lichens overgrown
Than anything which once could have been human.
And ever as she goes the palsied woman

   .   .   .   .   .

'How slow and painfully you seem to walk,
Poor Media! you tire yourself with talk.'
            'And well it may,
Fiordispina, dearest—well-a-day!
You are hastening to a marriage-bed;
I to the grave!'—'And if my love were dead,
Unless my heart deceives me, I would lie
Beside him in my shroud as willingly
As now in the gay night-dress Lilla wrought.'
'Fie, child! Let that unseasonable thought
Not be remembered till it snows in June;

FIORDISPINA

Such fancies are a music out of tune
With the sweet dance your heart must keep to-night.
What! would you take all beauty and delight
Back to the Paradise from which you sprung,
And leave to grosser mortals?—
And say, sweet lamb, would you not learn the sweet
And subtle mystery by which spirits meet?
Who knows whether the loving game is played,
When, once of mortal [vesture] disarrayed,
The naked soul goes wandering here and there
Through the wide deserts of Elysian air?
The violet dies not till it'—

1820.

FRAGMENT
PATER OMNIPOTENS

SERENE in his unconquerable might
  Endued, the Almighty King, his steadfast throne
Encompassed unapproachably with power
And darkness and deep solitude and awe
Stood like a black cloud on some aëry cliff
Embosoming its lightning—in his sight
Unnumbered glorious spirits trembling stood
Like slaves before their Lord—prostrate around
Heaven's multitudes hymned everlasting praise.

1820.

GINEVRA

WILD, pale, and wonder-stricken, even as one
Who staggers forth into the air and sun
From the dark chamber of a mortal fever,
Bewildered, and incapable, and ever
Fancying strange comments in her dizzy brain
Of usual shapes, till the familiar train
Of objects and of persons passed like things
Strange as a dreamer's mad imaginings,
Ginevra from the nuptial altar went;
The vows to which her lips had sworn assent
Rung in her brain still with a jarring din,
Deafening the lost intelligence within.

And so she moved under the bridal veil,
Which made the paleness of her cheek more pale,
And deepened the faint crimson of her mouth,
And darkened her dark locks, as moonlight doth, —
And of the gold and jewels glittering there
She scarce felt conscious, — but the weary glare
Lay like a chaos of unwelcome light,
Vexing the sense with gorgeous undelight,
A moonbeam in the shadow of a cloud
Was less heavenly fair — her face was bowed,
And as she passed, the diamonds in her hair

266

GINEVRA

Were mirrored in the polished marble stair
Which led from the cathedral to the street;
And ever as she went her light fair feet
Erased these images.

    The bride-maidens who round her thronging came,
Some with a sense of self-rebuke and shame,
Envying the unenviable; and others
Making the joy which should have been another's
Their own by gentle sympathy; and some
Sighing to think of an unhappy home:
Some few admiring what can ever lure
Maidens to leave the heaven serene and pure
Of parents' smiles for life's great cheat; a thing
Bitter to taste, sweet in imagining.

    But they are all dispersed—and, lo! she stands
Looking in idle grief on her white hands,
Alone within the garden now her own;
And through the sunny air, with jangling tone,
The music of the merry marriage-bells,
Killing the azure silence, sinks and swells;—
Absorbed like one within a dream who dreams
That he is dreaming, until slumber seems
A mockery of itself—when suddenly
Antonio stood before her, pale as she.

GINEVRA

With agony, with sorrow, and with pride,
He lifted his wan eyes upon the bride,
And said—'Is this thy faith?' and then as one
Whose sleeping face is stricken by the sun
With light like a harsh voice, which bids him rise
And look upon his day of life with eyes
Which weep in vain that they can dream no more,
Ginevra saw her lover, and forbore
To shriek or faint, and checked the stifling blood
Rushing upon her heart, and unsubdued
Said—'Friend, if earthly violence or ill,
Suspicion, doubt, or the tyrannic will
Of parents, chance or custom, time or change,
Or circumstance, or terror, or revenge,
Or wildered looks, or words, or evil speech,
With all their stings and venom can impeach
Our love,—we love not:—if the grave which hides
The victim from the tyrant, and divides
The cheek that whitens from the eyes that dart
Imperious inquisition to the heart
That is another's, could dissever ours,
We love not.'—'What! do not the silent hours
Beckon thee to Gherardi's bridal bed?
Is not that ring'—a pledge, he would have said,
Of broken vows, but she with patient look
The golden circle from her finger took,

268

GINEVRA

And said—'Accept this token of my faith,
The pledge of vows to be absolved by death;
And I am dead or shall be soon—my knell
Will mix its music with that merry bell.
Does it not sound as if they sweetly said
"We toll a corpse out of the marriage-bed"?
The flowers upon my bridal chamber strewn
Will serve unfaded for my bier—so soon
That even the dying violet will not die
Before Ginevra.' The strong fantasy
Had made her accents weaker and more weak,
And quenched the crimson life upon her cheek,
And glazed her eyes, and spread an atmosphere
Round her, which chilled the burning noon with fear,
Making her but an image of the thought
Which, like a prophet or a shadow, brought
News of the terrors of the coming time.
Like an accuser branded with the crime
He would have cast on a belovèd friend,
Whose dying eyes reproach not to the end
The pale betrayer—he then with vain repentance
Would share, he cannot now avert, the sentence—
Antonio stood and would have spoken, when
The compound voice of women and of men
Was heard approaching; he retired, while she
Was led amid the admiring company

GINEVRA

Back to the palace, —and her maidens soon
Changed her attire for the afternoon,
And left her at her own request to keep
An hour of quiet rest:—like one asleep
With open eyes and folded hands she lay,
Pale in the light of the declining day.

Meanwhile the day sinks fast, the sun is set,
And in the lighted hall the guests are met;
The beautiful looked lovelier in the light
Of love, and admiration, and delight
Reflected from a thousand hearts and eyes,
Kindling a momentary Paradise.
This crowd is safer than the silent wood,
Where love's own doubts disturb the solitude;
On frozen hearts the fiery rain of wine
Falls, and the dew of music more divine
Tempers the deep emotions of the time
To spirits cradled in a sunny clime:—
How many meet, who never yet have met,
To part too soon, but never to forget.
How many saw the beauty, power and wit
Of looks and words which ne'er enchanted yet;
But life's familiar veil was now withdrawn,
As the world leaps before an earthquake's dawn,
And unprophetic of the coming hours,

GINEVRA

The matin winds from the expanded flowers
Scatter their hoarded incense, and awaken
The earth, until the dewy sleep is shaken
From every living heart which it possesses,
Through seas and winds, cities and wildernesses,
As if the future and the past were all
Treasured i' the instant;—so Gherardi's hall
Laughed in the mirth of its lord's festival,
Till some one asked—'Where is the Bride?' And then
A bridesmaid went, —and ere she came again
A silence fell upon the guests—a pause
Of expectation, as when beauty awes
All hearts with its approach, though unbeheld;
Then wonder, and then fear that wonder quelled;—
For whispers passed from mouth to ear which drew
The colour from the hearer's cheeks, and flew
Louder and swifter round the company;
And then Gherardi entered with an eye
Of ostentatious trouble, and a crowd
Surrounded him, and some were weeping loud.

    They found Ginevra dead! if it be death
To lie without motion, or pulse, or breath,
With waxen cheeks, and limbs cold, stiff, and white,
And open eyes, whose fixed and glassy light
Mocked at the speculation they had owned.

GINEVRA

If it be death, when there is felt around
A smell of clay, a pale and icy glare,
And silence, and a sense that lifts the hair
From the scalp to the ankles, as it were
Corruption from the spirit passing forth,
And giving all it shrouded to the earth,
And leaving as swift lightning in its flight
Ashes, and smoke, and darkness: in our night
Of thought we know thus much of death, —no more
Than the unborn dream of our life before
Their barks are wrecked on its inhospitable shore.
The marriage feast and its solemnity
Was turned to funeral pomp—the company,
With heavy hearts and looks, broke up; nor they
Who loved the dead went weeping on their way
Alone, but sorrow mixed with sad surprise
Loosened the springs of pity in all eyes,
On which that form, whose fate they weep in vain,
Will never, thought they, kindle smiles again.
The lamps which, half extinguished in their haste,
Gleamed few and faint o'er the abandoned feast,
Showed as it were within the vaulted room
A cloud of sorrow hanging, as if gloom
Had passed out of men's minds into the air.
Some few yet stood around Gherardi there,
Friends and relations of the dead, —and he,

GINEVRA

A loveless man, accepted torpidly
The consolation that he wanted not;
Awe in the place of grief within him wrought.
Their whispers made the solemn silence seem
More still—some wept, ...
Some melted into tears without a sob,
And some with hearts that might be heard to throb
Leaned on the table, and at intervals
Shuddered to hear through the deserted halls
And corridors the thrilling shrieks which came
Upon the breeze of night, that shook the flame
Of every torch and taper as it swept
From out the chamber where the women kept;—
Their tears fell on the dear companion cold
Of pleasures now departed; then was knolled
The bell of death, and soon the priests arrived,
And finding Death their penitent had shrived,
Returned like ravens from a corpse whereon
A vulture has just feasted to the bone.
And then the mourning women came. —

.   .   .   .   .

THE DIRGE

Old winter was gone
In his weakness back to the mountains hoar,

GINEVRA

And the spring came down
From the planet that hovers upon the shore
  Where the sea of sunlight encroaches
On the limits of wintry night;—
If the land, and the air, and the sea,
  Rejoice not when spring approaches,
We did not rejoice in thee,
      Ginevra!

She is still, she is cold
     On the bridal couch,
One step to the white deathbed,
     And one to the bier,
And one to the charnel—and one, oh where?
     The dark arrow fled
     In the noon.

Ere the sun through heaven once more has rolled,
The rats in her heart
Will have made their nest,
And the worms be alive in her golden hair,
While the Spirit that guides the sun,
Sits throned in his flaming chair,
    She shall sleep.

1821.

THE ZUCCA

I

SUMMER was dead and Autumn was expiring,
And infant Winter laughed upon the land
All cloudlessly and cold;—when I, desiring
    More in this world than any understand,
Wept o'er the beauty, which, like sea retiring,
    Had left the earth bare as the wave-worn sand
Of my lorn heart, and o'er the grass and flowers
Pale for the falsehood of the flattering Hours.

2

Summer was dead, but I yet lived to weep
    The instability of all but weeping;
And on the Earth lulled in her winter sleep
    I woke, and envied her as she was sleeping.
Too happy Earth! over thy face shall creep
    The wakening vernal airs, until thou, leaping
From unremembered dreams, shalt   see
No death divide thy immortality.

3

I loved—oh, no, I mean not one of ye,
    Or any earthly one, though ye are dear
As human heart to human heart may be;—
    I loved, I know not what—but this low sphere

THE ZUCCA

And all that it contains, contains not thee,
   Thou, whom, seen nowhere, I feel everywhere.
From Heaven and Earth, and all that in them are,
Veiled art thou, like a   star.

4

By Heaven and Earth, from all whose shapes thou flowest,
   Neither to be contained, delayed, nor hidden;
Making divine the loftiest and the lowest,
   When for a moment thou art not forbidden
To live within the life which thou bestowest;
   And leaving noblest things vacant and chidden,
Cold as a corpse after the spirit's flight,
Blank as the sun after the birth of night.

5

In winds, and trees, and streams, and all things common,
   In music and the sweet unconscious tone
Of animals, and voices which are human,
   Meant to express some feelings of their own;
In the soft motions and rare smile of woman,
   In flowers and leaves, and in the grass fresh-shown,
Or dying in the autumn, I the most
Adore thee present or lament thee lost.

6

And thus I went lamenting, when I saw
   A plant upon the river's margin lie,

276

THE ZUCCA

Like one who loved beyond his nature's law,
    And in despair had cast him down to die;
Its leaves, which had outlived the frost, the thaw
    Had blighted; like a heart which hatred's eye
Can blast not, but which pity kills; the dew
Lay on its spotted leaves like tears too true.

7

The Heavens had wept upon it, but the Earth
    Had crushed it on her unmaternal breast

    .   .   .   .   .

8

I bore it to my chamber, and I planted
    It in a vase full of the lightest mould;
The winter beams which out of Heaven slanted
    Fell through the window-panes, disrobed of cold,
Upon its leaves and flowers; the stars which panted
    In evening for the Day, whose car has rolled
Over the horizon's wave, with looks of light
Smiled on it from the threshold of the night.

9

The mitigated influences of air
    And light revived the plant, and from it grew
Strong leaves and tendrils, and its flowers fair,
    Full as a cup with the vine's burning dew,
O'erflowed with golden colours; an atmosphere

THE ZUCCA

Of vital warmth enfolded it anew,
And every impulse sent to every part
The unbeheld pulsations of its heart.

10

Well might the plant grow beautiful and strong,
   Even if the air and sun had smiled not on it;
For one wept o'er it all the winter long
   Tears pure as Heaven's rain, which fell upon it
Hour after hour; for sounds of softest song
   Mixed with the stringèd melodies that won it
To leave the gentle lips on which it slept,
Had loosed the heart of him who sat and wept.

11

Had loosed his heart, and shook the leaves and flowers
   On which he wept, the while the savage storm
Waked by the darkest of December's hours
   Was raving round the chamber hushed and warm;
The birds were shivering in their leafless bowers,
   The fish were frozen in the pools, the form
Of every summer plant was dead . . .
Whilst this . . .

    ·   ·   ·   ·   ·

1822.

278

THE TRIUMPH OF LIFE

SWIFT as a spirit hastening to his task
Of glory and of good, the Sun sprang forth
Rejoicing in his splendour, and the mask

Of darkness fell from the awakened Earth—
The smokeless altars of the mountain snows
Flamed above crimson clouds, and at the birth

Of light, the Ocean's orison arose,
To which the birds tempered their matin lay.
All flowers in field or forest which unclose

Their trembling eyelids to the kiss of day,
Swinging their censers in the element,
With orient incense lit by the new ray

Burned slow and inconsumably, and sent
Their odorous sighs up to the smiling air;
And, in succession due, did continent,

Isle, ocean, and all things that in them wear
The form and character of mortal mould,
Rise as the Sun their father rose, to bear

Their portion of the toil, which he of old
Took as his own, and then imposed on them:
But I, whom thoughts which must remain untold

THE TRIUMPH OF LIFE

Had kept as wakeful as the stars that gem
The cone of night, now they were laid asleep
Stretched my faint limbs beneath the hoary stem

Which an old chestnut flung athwart the steep
Of a green Apennine: before me fled
The night; behind me rose the day; the deep

Was at my feet, and Heaven above my head, —
When a strange trance over my fancy grew
Which was not slumber, for the shade it spread

Was so transparent, that the scene came through
As clear as when a veil of light is drawn
O'er evening hills they glimmer; and I knew

That I had felt the freshness of that dawn
Bathe in the same cold dew my brow and hair,
And sate as thus upon that slope of lawn

Under the self-same bough, and heard as there
The birds, the fountains and the ocean hold
Sweet talk in music through the enamoured air,
And then a vision on my brain was rolled.

*

As in that trance of wondrous thought I lay,
This was the tenour of my waking dream: —
Methought I sate beside a public way

THE TRIUMPH OF LIFE

Thick strewn with summer dust, and a great stream
Of people there was hurrying to and fro,
Numerous as gnats upon the evening gleam,

All hastening onward, yet none seemed to know
Whither he went, or whence he came, or why
He made one of the multitude, and so

Was borne amid the crowd, as through the sky
One of the million leaves of summer's bier;
Old age and youth, manhood and infancy,

Mixed in one mighty torrent did appear,
Some flying from the thing they feared, and some
Seeking the object of another's fear;

And others, as with steps towards the tomb,
Pored on the trodden worms that crawled beneath,
And others mournfully within the gloom

Of their own shadow walked, and called it death;
And some fled from it as it were a ghost,
Half fainting in the affliction of vain breath:

But more, with motions which each other crossed,
Pursued or shunned the shadows the clouds threw,
Or birds within the noonday aether lost,

Upon that path where flowers never grew, —
And, weary with vain toil and faint for thirst,
Heard not the fountains, whose melodious dew

THE TRIUMPH OF LIFE

Out of their mossy cells forever burst;
Nor felt the breeze which from the forest told
Of grassy paths and wood-lawns interspersed

With overarching elms and caverns cold,
And violet banks where sweet dreams brood, but they
Pursued their serious folly as of old.

And as I gazed, methought that in the way
The throng grew wilder, as the woods of June
When the south wind shakes the extinguished day,

And a cold glare, intenser than the noon,
But icy cold, obscured with blinding light
The sun, as he the stars. Like the young moon—

When on the sunlit limits of the night
Her white shell trembles amid crimson air,
And whilst the sleeping tempest gathers might—

Doth, as the herald of its coming, bear
The ghost of its dead mother, whose dim form
Bends in dark aether from her infant's chair, —

So came a chariot on the silent storm
Of its own rushing splendour, and a Shape
So sate within, as one whom years deform,

Beneath a dusky hood and double cape,
Crouching within the shadow of a tomb;
And o'er what seemed the head a cloud-like crape

THE TRIUMPH OF LIFE

Was bent, a dun and faint aethereal gloom
Tempering the light. Upon the chariot-beam
A Janus-visaged Shadow did assume

The guidance of that wonder-wingèd team;
The shapes which drew it in thick lightenings
Were lost:—I heard alone on the air's soft stream

The music of their ever-moving wings.
All the four faces of that Charioteer
Had their eyes banded; little profit brings

Speed in the van and blindness in the rear,
Nor then avail the beams that quench the sun, —
Or that with banded eyes could pierce the sphere

Of all that is, has been or will be done;
So ill was the car guided—but it passed
With solemn speed majestically on.

The crowd gave way, and I arose aghast,
Or seemed to rise, so mighty was the trance,
And saw, like clouds upon the thunder-blast,

The million with fierce song and maniac dance
Raging around—such seemed the jubilee
As when to greet some conqueror's advance

Imperial Rome poured forth her living sea
From senate-house, and forum, and theatre,
When   upon the free

THE TRIUMPH OF LIFE

Had bound a yoke, which soon they stooped to bear.
Nor wanted here the just similitude
Of a triumphal pageant, for where'er

The chariot rolled, a captive multitude
Was driven;—all those who had grown old in power
Or misery,—all who had their age subdued

By action or by suffering, and whose hour
Was drained to its last sand in weal or woe,
So that the trunk survived both fruit and flower;—

All those whose fame or infamy must grow
Till the great winter lay the form and name
Of this green earth with them for ever low;—

All but the sacred few who could not tame
Their spirits to the conquerors—but as soon
As they had touched the world with living flame,

Fled back like eagles to their native noon,
Or those who put aside the diadem
Of earthly thrones or gems . . .

Were there, of Athens or Jerusalem,
Were neither mid the mighty captives seen,
Nor mid the ribald crowd that followed them,

Nor those who went before fierce and obscene.
The wild dance maddens in the van, and those
Who lead it—fleet as shadows on the green,

THE TRIUMPH OF LIFE

Outspeed the chariot, and without repose
Mix with each other in tempestuous measure
To savage music, wilder as it grows,

They, tortured by their agonizing pleasure,
Convulsed and on the rapid whirlwinds spun
Of that fierce Spirit, whose unholy leisure

Was soothed by mischief since the world begun,
Throw back their heads and loose their streaming hair;
And in their dance round her who dims the sun,

Maidens and youths fling their wild arms in air
As their feet twinkle; they recede, and now
Bending within each other's atmosphere,

Kindle invisibly—and as they glow,
Like moths by light attracted and repelled,
Oft to their bright destruction come and go,

Till like two clouds into one vale impelled,
That shake the mountains when their lightnings mingle
And die in rain—the fiery band which held

Their natures, snaps—while the shock still may tingle
One falls and then another in the path
Senseless—nor is the desolation single,

Yet ere I can say *where*—the chariot hath
Passed over them—nor other trace I find
But as of foam after the ocean's wrath

THE TRIUMPH OF LIFE

Is spent upon the desert shore;—behind,
Old men and women foully disarrayed,
Shake their gray hairs in the insulting wind,

And follow in the dance, with limbs decayed,
Seeking to reach the light which leaves them still
Farther behind and deeper in the shade.

But not the less with impotence of will
They wheel, though ghastly shadows interpose
Round them and round each other, and fulfil

Their work, and in the dust from whence they rose
Sink, and corruption veils them as they lie,
And past in these performs what   in those.

Struck to the heart by this sad pageantry,
Half to myself I said—'And what is this?
Whose shape is that within the car? And why—'

I would have added—'is all here amiss?—'
But a voice answered—'Life!'—I turned, and knew
(O Heaven, have mercy on such wretchedness!)

That what I thought was an old root which grew
To strange distortion out of the hill side,
Was indeed one of those deluded crew,

And that the grass, which methought hung so wide
And white, was but his thin discoloured hair,
And that the holes he vainly sought to hide,

286

THE TRIUMPH OF LIFE

Were or had been eyes:—'If thou canst forbear
To join the dance, which I had well forborne,'
Said the grim Feature, of my thought aware,

'I will unfold that which to this deep scorn
Led me and my companions, and relate
The progress of the pageant since the morn;

'If thirst of knowledge shall not then abate,
Follow it thou even to the night, but I
Am weary.'—Then like one who with the weight

Of his own words is staggered, wearily
He paused; and ere he could resume, I cried:
'First, who art thou?'—'Before thy memory,

'I feared, loved, hated, suffered, did and died,
And if the spark with which Heaven lit my spirit
Had been with purer nutriment supplied,

'Corruption would not now thus much inherit
Of what was once Rousseau,—nor this disguise
Stain that which ought to have disdained to wear it;

'If I have been extinguished, yet there rise
A thousand beacons from the spark I bore'—
'And who are those chained to the car?'—'The wise,

'The great, the unforgotten,—they who wore
Mitres and helms and crowns, or wreaths of light,
Signs of thought's empire over thought—their lore

THE TRIUMPH OF LIFE

'Taught them not this, to know themselves; their might
Could not repress the mystery within,
And for the morn of truth they feigned, deep night

'Caught them ere evening.'—'Who is he with chin
Upon his breast, and hands crossed on his chain?'—
'The child of a fierce hour; he sought to win

'The world, and lost all that it did contain
Of greatness, in its hope destroyed; and more
Of fame and peace than virtue's self can gain

'Without the opportunity which bore
Him on its eagle pinions to the peak
From which a thousand climbers have before

'Fallen, as Napoleon fell.'—I felt my cheek
Alter, to see the shadow pass away,
Whose grasp had left the giant world so weak

That every pigmy kicked it as it lay;
And much I grieved to think how power and will
In opposition rule our mortal day,

And why God made irreconcilable
Good and the means of good; and for despair
I half disdained mine eyes' desire to fill

With the spent vision of the times that were
And scarce have ceased to be.—'Dost thou behold,'
Said my guide, 'those spoilers spoiled, Voltaire,

THE TRIUMPH OF LIFE

'Frederick, and Paul, Catherine, and Leopold,
And hoary anarchs, demagogues, and sage—
   names which the world thinks always old,

'For in the battle Life and they did wage,
She remained conqueror. I was overcome
By my own heart alone, which neither age,

'Nor tears, nor infamy, nor now the tomb
Could temper to its object.'—'Let them pass,'
I cried, 'the world and its mysterious doom

'Is not so much more glorious than it was,
That I desire to worship those who drew
New figures on its false and fragile glass

'As the old faded.'—'Figures ever new
Rise on the bubble, paint them as you may;
We have but thrown, as those before us threw,

'Our shadows on it as it passed away.
But mark how chained to the triumphal chair
The mighty phantoms of an elder day;

'All that is mortal of great Plato there
Expiates the joy and woe his master knew not;
The star that ruled his doom was far too fair.

'And life, where long that flower of Heaven grew not,
Conquered that heart by love, which gold, or pain,
Or age, or sloth, or slavery could subdue not.

THE TRIUMPH OF LIFE

'And near him walk the   twain,
The tutor and his pupil, whom Dominion
Followed as tame as vulture in a chain.

'The world was darkened beneath either pinion
Of him whom from the flock of conquerors
Fame singled out for her thunder-bearing minion;

'The other long outlived both woes and wars,
Throned in the thoughts of men, and still had kept
The jealous key of Truth's eternal doors,

'If Bacon's eagle spirit had not lept
Like lightning out of darkness—he compelled
The Proteus shape of Nature, as it slept

'To wake, and lead him to the caves that held
The treasure of the secrets of its reign.
See the great bards of elder time, who quelled

'The passions which they sung, as by their strain
May well be known: their living melody
Tempers its own contagion to the vein

'Of those who are infected with it—I
Have suffered what I wrote, or viler pain!
And so my words have seeds of misery—

'Even as the deeds of others, not as theirs.'
And then he pointed to a company,

THE TRIUMPH OF LIFE

'Midst whom I quickly recognized the heirs
Of Caesar's crime, from him to Constantine;
The anarch chiefs, whose force and murderous snares

Had founded many a sceptre-bearing line,
And spread the plague of gold and blood abroad:
And Gregory and John, and men divine,

Who rose like shadows between man and God;
Till that eclipse, still hanging over heaven,
Was worshipped by the world o'er which they strode,

For the true sun it quenched—'Their power was given
But to destroy,' replied the leader:—'I
Am one of those who have created, even

'If it be but a world of agony.'—
'Whence camest thou? and whither goest thou?
How did thy course begin?' I said, 'and why?

'Mine eyes are sick of this perpetual flow
Of people, and my heart sick of one sad thought—
Speak!'—'Whence I am, I partly seem to know,

'And how and by what paths I have been brought
To this dread pass, methinks even thou mayst guess;—
Why this should be, my mind can compass not;

'Whither the conqueror hurries me, still less;—
But follow thou, and from spectator turn
Actor or victim in this wretchedness,

THE TRIUMPH OF LIFE

'And what thou wouldst be taught I then may learn
From thee. Now listen:—In the April prime,
When all the forest-tips began to burn

'With kindling green, touched by the azure clime
Of the young season, I was laid asleep
Under a mountain, which from unknown time

'Had yawned into a cavern, high and deep;
And from it came a gentle rivulet,
Whose water, like clear air, in its calm sweep

'Bent the soft grass, and kept for ever wet
The stems of the sweet flowers, and filled the grove
With sounds, which whoso hears must needs forget

'All pleasure and all pain, all hate and love,
Which they had known before that hour of rest;
A sleeping mother then would dream not of

'Her only child who died upon the breast
At eventide—a king would mourn no more
The crown of which his brows were dispossessed

'When the sun lingered o'er his ocean floor
To gild his rival's new prosperity.
Thou wouldst forget thus vainly to deplore

'Ills, which if ills can find no cure from thee,
The thought of which no other sleep will quell,
Nor other music blot from memory,

THE TRIUMPH OF LIFE

'So sweet and deep is the oblivious spell;
And whether life had been before that sleep
The Heaven which I imagine, or a Hell

'Like this harsh world in which I woke to weep,
I know not. I arose, and for a space
The scene of woods and waters seemed to keep,

'Though it was now broad day, a gentle trace
Of light diviner than the common sun
Sheds on the common earth, and all the place

'Was filled with magic sounds woven into one
Oblivious melody, confusing sense
Amid the gliding waves and shadows dun;

'And, as I looked, the bright omnipresence
Of morning through the orient cavern flowed,
And the sun's image radiantly intense

'Burned on the waters of the well that glowed
Like gold, and threaded all the forest's maze
With winding paths of emerald fire; there stood

'Amid the sun, as he amid the blaze
Of his own glory, on the vibrating
Floor of the fountain, paved with flashing rays,

'A Shape all light, which with one hand did fling
Dew on the earth, as if she were the dawn,
And the invisible rain did ever sing

THE TRIUMPH OF LIFE

'A silver music on the mossy lawn;
And still before me on the dusky grass,
Iris her many-coloured scarf had drawn:

'In her right hand she bore a crystal glass,
Mantling with bright Nepenthe; the fierce splendour
Fell from her as she moved under the mass

'Of the deep cavern, and with palms so tender,
Their tread broke not the mirror of its billow,
Glided along the river, and did bend her

'Head under the dark boughs, till like a willow
Her fair hair swept the bosom of the stream
That whispered with delight to be its pillow.

'As one enamoured is upborne in dream
O'er lily-paven lakes, mid silver mist,
To wondrous music, so this shape might seem

'Partly to tread the waves with feet which kissed
The dancing foam; partly to glide along
The air which roughened the moist amethyst,

'Or the faint morning beams that fell among
The trees, or the soft shadows of the trees;
And her feet, ever to the ceaseless song

'Of leaves, and winds, and waves, and birds, and bees,
And falling drops, moved in a measure new
Yet sweet, as on the summer evening breeze,

THE TRIUMPH OF LIFE

'Up from the lake a shape of golden dew
Between two rocks, athwart the rising moon,
Dances i' the wind, where never eagle flew;

'And still her feet, no less than the sweet tune
To which they moved, seemed as they moved to blot
The thoughts of him who gazed on them; and soon

'All that was, seemed as if it had been not;
And all the gazer's mind was strewn beneath
Her feet like embers; and she, thought by thought,

'Trampled its sparks into the dust of death
As day upon the threshold of the east
Treads out the lamps of night, until the breath

'Of darkness re-illumine even the least
Of heaven's living eyes—like day she came,
Making the night a dream; and ere she ceased

'To move, as one between desire and shame
Suspended, I said—If, as it doth seem,
Thou comest from the realm without a name

'Into this valley of perpetual dream,
Show whence I came, and where I am, and why—
Pass not away upon the passing stream.

'Arise and quench thy thirst, was her reply.
And as a shut lily stricken by the wand
Of dewy morning's vital alchemy,

THE TRIUMPH OF LIFE

'I rose; and, bending at her sweet command,
Touched with faint lips the cup she raised,
And suddenly my brain became as sand

'Where the first wave had more than half erased
The track of deer on desert Labrador;
Whilst the wolf, from which they fled amazed,

'Leaves his stamp visibly upon the shore,
Until the second bursts;—so on my sight
Burst a new vision, never seen before,

'And the fair shape waned in the coming light,
As veil by veil the silent splendour drops
From Lucifer, amid the chrysolite

'Of sunrise, ere it tinge the mountain-tops;
And as the presence of that fairest planet,
Although unseen, is felt by one who hopes

'That his day's path may end as he began it,
In that star's smile, whose light is like the scent
Of a jonquil when evening breezes fan it,

'Or the soft note in which his dear lament
The Brescian shepherd breathes, or the caress
That turned his weary slumber to content;

'So knew I in that light's severe excess
The presence of that Shape which on the stream
Moved, as I moved along the wilderness,

THE TRIUMPH OF LIFE

'More dimly than a day-appearing dream,
The ghost of a forgotten form of sleep;
A light of heaven, whose half-extinguished beam

'Through the sick day in which we wake to weep
Glimmers, for ever sought, for ever lost;
So did that shape its obscure tenour keep

'Beside my path, as silent as a ghost;
But the new Vision, and the cold bright car,
With solemn speed and stunning music, crossed

'The forest, and as if from some dread war
Triumphantly returning, the loud million
Fiercely extolled the fortune of her star.

'A moving arch of victory, the vermilion
And green and azure plumes of Iris had
Built high over her wind-wingèd pavilion,

'And underneath aethereal glory clad
The wilderness, and far before her flew
The tempest of the splendour, which forbade

'Shadow to fall from leaf and stone; the crew
Seemed in that light, like atomies to dance
Within a sunbeam;—some upon the new

'Embroidery of flowers, that did enhance
The grassy vesture of the desert, played,
Forgetful of the chariot's swift advance;

THE TRIUMPH OF LIFE

'Others stood gazing, till within the shade
Of the great mountain its light left them dim;
Others outspeeded it; and others made

'Circles around it, like the clouds that swim
Round the high moon in a bright sea of air;
And more did follow, with exulting hymn,

'The chariot and the captives fettered there:—
But all like bubbles on an eddying flood
Fell into the same track at last, and were

'Borne onward.—I among the multitude
Was swept—me, sweetest flowers delayed not long;
Me, not the shadow nor the solitude;

'Me, not that falling stream's Lethean song;
Me, not the phantom of that early Form
Which moved upon its motion—but among

'The thickest billows of that living storm
I plunged, and bared my bosom to the clime
Of that cold light, whose airs too soon deform.

'Before the chariot had begun to climb
The opposing steep of that mysterious dell,
Behold a wonder worthy of the rhyme

'Of him who from the lowest depths of hell,
Through every paradise and through all glory,
Love led serene, and who returned to tell

298

THE TRIUMPH OF LIFE

'The words of hate and awe; the wondrous story
How all things are transfigured except Love;
For deaf as is a sea, which wrath makes hoary,

'The world can hear not the sweet notes that move
The sphere whose light is melody to lovers—
A wonder worthy of his rhyme. — The grove

'Grew dense with shadows to its inmost covers,
The earth was gray with phantoms, and the air
Was peopled with dim forms, as when there hovers

'A flock of vampire-bats before the glare
Of the tropic sun, bringing, ere evening,
Strange night upon some Indian isle;—thus were

'Phantoms diffused around; and some did fling
Shadows of shadows, yet unlike themselves,
Behind them; some like eaglets on the wing

'Were lost in the white day; others like elves
Danced in a thousand unimagined shapes
Upon the sunny streams and grassy shelves;

'And others sate chattering like restless apes
On vulgar hands, . . .
Some made a cradle of the ermined capes

'Of kingly mantles; some across the tiar
Of pontiffs sate like vultures; others played
Under the crown which girt with empire

THE TRIUMPH OF LIFE

'A baby's or an idiot's brow, and made
Their nests in it. The old anatomies
Sate hatching their bare broods under the shade

'Of daemon wings, and laughed from their dead eyes
To reassume the delegated power,
Arrayed in which those worms did monarchize,

'Who made this earth their charnel. Others more
Humble, like falcons, sate upon the fist
Of common men, and round their heads did soar;

'Or like small gnats and flies, as thick as mist
On evening marshes, thronged about the brow
Of lawyers, statesmen, priest and theorist;—

'And others, like discoloured flakes of snow
On fairest bosoms and the sunniest hair,
Fell, and were melted by the youthful glow

'Which they extinguished; and, like tears, they were
A veil to those from whose faint lids they rained
In drops of sorrow. I became aware

'Of whence those forms proceeded which thus stained
The track in which we moved. After brief space,
From every form the beauty slowly waned;

'From every firmest limb and fairest face
The strength and freshness fell like dust, and left
The action and the shape without the grace

THE TRIUMPH OF LIFE

'Of life. The marble brow of youth was cleft
With care; and in those eyes where once hope shone,
Desire, like a lioness bereft

'Of her last cub, glared ere it died; each one
Of that great crowd sent forth incessantly
These shadows, numerous as the dead leaves blown

'In autumn evening from a poplar tree.
Each like himself and like each other were
At first; but some distorted seemed to be

'Obscure clouds, moulded by the casual air;
And of this stuff the car's creative ray
Wrought all the busy phantoms that were there,

'As the sun shapes the clouds; thus on the way
Mask after mask fell from the countenance
And form of all; and long before the day

'Was old, the joy which waked like heaven's glance
The sleepers in the oblivious valley, died;
And some grew weary of the ghastly dance,

'And fell, as I have fallen, by the wayside;—
Those soonest from whose forms most shadows passed,
And least of strength and beauty did abide.

'Then, what is life? I cried.'—

1822.

www.ingramcontent.com/pod-product-compliance
Lightning Source LLC
Chambersburg PA
CBHW031944080426
42735CB00007B/253